Occasional & Joke Poems

Also by Alistair Noon

COLLECTIONS
Earth Records
The Kerosene Singing

CHAPBOOKS
At the Emptying of Dustbins
In People's Park
Animals and Places
Some Questions on the Cultural Revolution
Out of the Cave
Across the Water
Swamp Area
Long & Other Short Poems
Surveyors' Riddles *(with Giles Goodland)*
QUAD
Neptune All Night
Two Verse Essays

AS TRANSLATOR
Alexander Pushkin, *The Bronze Horseman*
Monika Rinck, *Sixteen Poems*
August Stramm, *The Last Drop*
Osip Mandelstam, *Concert at a Railway Station: Selected Poems*
Osip Mandelstam, *The Voronezh Workbooks*
Ilia Kitup, various pamphlets

Osip Mandelstam

Occasional & Joke Poems

*translated from Russian
by Alistair Noon*

Shearsman Books

First published in the United Kingdom in 2022 by
Shearsman Books
P O Box 4239
Swindon
SN3 9FN

Shearsman Books Ltd Registered Office
30–31 St. James Place, Mangotsfield, Bristol BS16 9JB
(this address not for correspondence)

www.shearsman.com

ISBN 978-1-84861-836-7

Translation copyright © Alistair Noon, 2022.

The right of Alistair Noon to be identified as the translator of this work
has been asserted by him in accordance with the
Copyrights, Designs and Patents Act of 1988.
All rights reserved.

Acknowledgements

Five of the 'Fables' were published on *Litter*, with thanks to Alan Baker. 'The Marguletics' were published in *The Fortnightly Review*, with thanks to Peter Riley and Denis Boyles. Some of the translations in this book appeared previously in *Concert at a Railway Station: Selected Poems* (Bristol: Shearsman Books, 2018), and before that in the journals acknowledged in that volume.

Contents

Translator's note   9
A Village of Poets   10

Occasional and Joke Poems

To a Man Who Acted a Spaniard ('A Riddle Unravelled')   31
If I'm honest with you   31
To be like a toy, that's what you'd change   32
Blok   32
The cow is chomping its hay   33
I'm closer to Acmeists by the Winter Palace   34
Pastoral   35
It's 1912, and the powers have ordained   36
I hear the conjugations' bells   37
He was automatic, polite but hard   37
Don't look glum   38
God, what a squeak! It's so bad it   38
Chumpties   39
An Anthology of Ancient Nonsense   40
Baron Emil grabs a knife   42
To improve her hair strength, one lady   42
That is Altmann. He is painter   43
There's a milk on which Pallas and I both feed   43
One morning, Sergeant Stutter   44
You're breathing into my trumpet, young man!   44
Yes it was twenty thousand I owed you!   44
Pushkin got given an avenue. Fiery old Lermontov too   45
The Fallen Officer (A Ballad)   46
Archangel Michael passed straight through   47
(…) Kandelaki's aide, Brekhnichov by name   47
So many crafts a man might practise   48

[From Dmitri Shepelenko's notebooks]
   Poets just don't give a shit!   49
   No silk for us but only wool   49
   Your heart is alive as such   49

As a teen, I minded the stripes of my modest mattress   50
Aphorisms on the Nonsense of Life   50
[Translations from Jules Romains's novel *Les Copains*]   53
The Ballad of the Gorlin   55
The Party let Publius in as a youth, to its golden ranks   57
You may not have known this before   58
The fact that Maria's that gullible should have been clear to me   59
Sonnet   60
Who's Mayakovsky's nemesis   61
I found my feet back here in your flat   62
But I love your streaks of grey   63
A bearing and a ball   64
Pomponych, civis *of Rome*   64
Visionary raving from Sinai to Tabor   65
Ubi bene, ibi patria, ancients tend   65
Some Jew in the Junior Communists chose   66

[Two poems on fur]
   She's long been huntin' Siberian furs, has Mrs. Karanovich   66
   I'd love to, Granny K   67

Lo! In Khalatov The Caliph's gardens   67

[The Vermel poems]
   Epigram in tercets   68
   Huffing and puffing, to and fro   69
   "I despair of Moscow and I have   69
   Vermel knew all the cantilevers   70
   Requiring a hat, Vermel went down   70
   His sleep is serene   70

A stallion meowed, a tomcat neighed   71

The Prince of Zvenigorod (fourteenth century)	71
The Marguletics	72
Margulis the Old would sing us	75
Young Manuilov, round he goes	75
Not as a wave on some Greek sea	75
I'm a man who's not from here	76
How long's it been now since GUM sold	76
Where the wilds went over to arable	77
The waters of Phlegethon lap	78
I hear Pyast's rapid steps on the stairs	79
Two translators once fell upon us	79
The old apocryphon that I recall	80
She's sitting there with well-parched lips	81
The Bolsheviks love lifts: a fact	82
That isn't the tail of a foal in a fit	84
I'd so like to see you a few decades later	85
The keeper comes, they buzz their wings	86
Along the shores of seas	87
Enamel, diamonds, plus some gold	88
I don't need any church in Rome	89
The errors of ears in keeping abreast	90
That young runt's a right mimosa	90
The fount of tears has frozen, three stone those shackles weigh	91
Natasha's asleep. A zephyr flies	92
Rural family size is big	93
Lena and Nora erupt like Etna	94
[Four-liners to Natasha Shtempel]	
Natasha's back, but where's she been?	95
If God dropped by and thus he spake	95
"Natasha, how would you spell nitwit?"	95
Oh Natasha, how clumsy of me	95
Natasha's ordered the next epigram	96
A savings-book Trosha has swiped from a library	96
Out of respect for the girl in the maid, the lad took his time	97
Decision	97

Relieved of all tasks when the truth was revealed	98
As in the primates, there's something which you	98
Gabriel Bloggs adored cigarettes	99
"Is it all quiet down there in the Balkans?"	99

Fables
    Once a sub-colonel, ex-White Guards   100
    The Fibber and the Fathers   101
    It seems that they've become so rare, oh   101
    Auntie and Mirabeau   102
    Dante and the Cabby   103
    There once was a son of a priest   104
    A farmer from a mudbrick farm   104
    Some citizen neither totally plastered   105
    A tailor with a decent head   105

Translator's note

All translations in the introduction and notes, of poems or prose either by Mandelstam or others, are either excerpted from *Concert at a Railway Station* (Bristol: Shearsman Books, 2018) or have been newly translated for this book.

Mandelstam poems referenced in the introduction or notes are referred to by the translation of their title or first line in either *Concert at a Railway Station* or *The Voronezh Workbooks* (Bristol: Shearsman Books, 2022). All websites cited were last accessed on 27 April 2021.

Essentially, the translations follow Alexander Mets's edition *Polnoye sobraniye sochineniy i pisem v tryokh tomakh*, vol. 1 (Moscow: Progress-Pleyada, 2009), while also referring to the earlier *Sochineniya v dvukh tomakh*, vol. 1 (Moscow: Khudozhestvennaya literatura, 1990), compiled by Pavel Nerler, with notes by the latter and A.D. Mikhailov, to all of whom I am indebted. Much of the information in my notes is drawn from these two editions. Further information was obtained from the invaluable *Mandelstam Encyclopedia* (in Russian) published by the Mandelstam Society under the general editorship of Nerler and the equally indefatigable Mandelstamologist Oleg Lekmanov, an enormous effort living up to its name (though any updated future edition might be encouraged to rescue as many obscure female figures as it does obscure male figures). I am very grateful to its editors and contributors, as well as to the anonymous editors and contributors of pertinent Wikipedia pages. Ralph Dutli's translations of many of these poems into German, demonstrating an enviable knowledge of Russian idioms, sensitivity to puns, and rooting out of information that Russian editors have passed over also helped me out of more than one conundrum. Dutli's German biography of Mandelstam remains illuminating and unavailable in English at the time of going to press. Ilia Kitup and Ksenya Kumm's clarifications over coffees, beers and emails have been an invaluable help to me and a worthwhile conviviality in their own right. I am very grateful for Kelvin Corcoran's guidance and feedback, Justin Quinn's critique and encouragement, and Sabine Heurs's support and understanding. All shortcomings remain, it goes without saying, my own.

A Village of Poets

I

More than one Mandelstam exists in the minds of those who've read his poems and prose and know something of his life. There's the writer of austerely classical verse around the time of the First World War. Then there's the recorder of the early years of the Soviet Union, fighting a rearguard action in the 1920s against those who would subsume literature to the needs of the State, enemies of the Open Society in Karl Popper's later terms. No later than the 1930s, we have the lonely, kenotic resister against Stalinism, though as post-Soviet critics have pointed out, also looking for an exit strategy as his income dried up and the Great Terror loomed. Most of the well-known photos of Mandelstam evoke and perpetuate such characterizations of him, conveying serenity at times and grimness at others. The literary historian and later critical memoirist Emma Gerstein's firsthand depiction of Mandelstam complicates these images further, plausibly revealing the reverse sides of his attested qualities of sensitivity, sincerity and self-assuredness, namely irascibility, demandingness and haughtiness.[1]

Mandelstam seems to have been all of these figures. But in parallel, he was also a producer of occasional verse, frequently humorous and mostly short: for a poet known to have composed much lengthier and weightier work in his head, this shorter and lighter poetry must have come comparatively spontaneously to him. This book aims to expand our view of Mandelstam in English with a comprehensive presentation of this verse. Perhaps "more or less comprehensive" would be more accurate, because it is in the nature of such pieces – sometimes composed *extempore* and mostly unpublished at the time of their writing – that the tundra reveals new specimens after decades in the memoirs or memories of their dedicatees or preservers, or that the DNA of texts already in glass cabinets is re-examined and their authorship questioned. For her husband's "serious" work, Nadezhda Mandelstam acted as poetry secretary, diligently setting down final written copies as poems were deemed finished (she would later manage the preservation of the late poems through distribution of copies to trusted individuals and her own memorization of them, and still later play an editorial role in their publication).[2] In contrast, this occasional work seems to have been flung

---

[1] *Moscow Memoirs*, translated by John Crowfoot (London: Harvill Press, 2004).

[2] Two facts suggest that her contribution to the writing process may have

to the wind, only for the seeds to take root, flower, and return their pollen much later. Nadezhda Mandelstam states explicitly in her memoirs that the couple seldom recorded these poems; in essence, therefore, the enemy of these pieces' preservation was not the NKVD (as was the case with Mandelstam's entire late "serious" work) but the Mandelstam poetry team itself.[3]

Mandelstam's fluent technique is always evident in these poems, and for their addressees, subjects or co-authors, they too were worth preserving. Their survival reveals – if on a humbler scale, and with less single-mindedness – a number of secondary Nadezhdas in this respect. These include not only Gerstein and Mandelstam's close friend and poetic ally Anna Akhmatova, but also lesser-known figures such as Yekaterina Livshits (widow of the Futurist poet Benedikt Livshits), the poet and journalist Maria Shkapskaya, and the writer Alexander Ivich, one of those to whom Nadezhda entrusted Mandelstam's late "serious" work. Another was Pavel Luknitsky, one of Mandelstam's neighbours at the House of the Arts in Petrograd in 1920/1921, a particularly fertile period for this kind of verse, and several of these neighbours (very immediate neighbours, given the housing conditions of the time) make an appearance here.[4] More individuals than these were involved, however, and just as the late "serious" work of Mandelstam is in a state of textual flux, these poems, spanning his entire writing life, cannot be pinned on the wall without some wriggling. In many cases, dedications, titles and variants were included or not according to their collectors' errors, knowledge or whims, making textual finality an impossibility.

Such humorous verse continued into the Voronezh period of internal exile (1934 to 1937) in which Osip and Nadezhda Mandelstam faced

---

gone beyond merely recording the poems. The first is her close knowledge of their writing, evident from her memoirs. The second is a comment by Anna Akhmatova in her *Pages from a Diary on Osip Mandelstam*, according to which "[Osip] asked [Nadezhda's] advice about every word in his poems". Akhmatova's hyperbolic remark is followed by the adjurement that this is backed up by Osip's letters to Nadezhda, which to this translator's reading is not really the case (unless there are letters that have escaped Mets's editorship), but the thrust of Akhmatova's point is clear.

[3] *Hope Abandoned*, translated by Max Hayward (Harmondsworth: Penguin Books, 1976), p. 149. Further references to Nadezhda Mandelstam's memoirs are to this and the first volume, with the same translator, *Hope Against Hope* (London: Collins and Harvill Press, 1971).

[4] See further notes in this book for more information on each of these figures.

ostracism, the threat of re-arrest, chronic housing problems, nutritional insecurity, and life-threatening medical issues. The verse of this period was sometimes addressed to (and preserved by) Natasha Shtempel, the young teacher who did much to alleviate or mitigate some of these problems. "In sinister times / there will also be singing", Brecht wrote around this time, and it seems there could even be laughing.[5] This verse seems to have stopped though – or perhaps was composed but lost – in the hyper-nomadic period between the end of Mandelstam's exile in Voronezh and his final arrest and transportation eastwards. At this point, there may have been no more laughing to be had.

Before that period of isolation, and in stark contrast to its enforced loneliness, the poems give a glimpse of a particular poetic subculture, of exchange and conviviality, with poems composed round restaurant tables, written in nonsense genres, recorded in scrapbooks, and enclosed in letters. The conviviality was in some cases only semi-voluntary: the poems born of the Mandelstams shacking up with others or others shacking up with the Mandelstams reflect the acute housing shortages of the time (which never really went away in the Soviet Union, despite the later massive house-building programmes under Khrushchev). In these poems, the reader will meet some of Mandelstam's poetic peers of schools diverse – Anna Akhmatova, Alexander Blok and Vladimir Mayakovsky – as well as less prominent Acmeists, Symbolists and Futurists (more on these groupings below), plus historians, biologists, politicians, editors and even humble translators. Not to forget a cleaner at one of the state-run writers' colonies Mandelstam lived in temporarily, and a fur-obsessed landlady. Not least, there are poems to some of the women towards whom Mandelstam made advances, including Maria Petrovykh and Natasha Shtempel (Nadezhda Mandelstam really did have a lot to put up with). The conviviality is cross-historical, extending to jocular treatments of historical poets who Mandelstam otherwise took seriously, such as Dante Alighieri (exiled from Florence) and André Chénier (guillotined in Paris), and more than once borrowing the epigramality of Catullus and the irony of Heine. Prose writers such as Flaubert, the Goncourt brothers and Maxim Gorky get cameos. The conviviality is also translocal: some of the poems were preserved by Russian emigrants in the post-revolutionary diaspora, while not a few of the figures in the poems were members of the Soviet Union's numerous nationalities.

The very occasionality and conviviality of this verse give the lie to the

---

[5] Bertolt Brecht, Motto to Part II of the Svendborg Poems, 1939.

post-Romantic myth of the poet as a lonely genius whose work arises in splendid isolation. In Mandelstam's case, this view is already attenuated by the role that Nadezhda Mandelstam played in the late poetry's textual fixing and subsequent survival, and more arguably by that of Sergei Rudakov as a sounding board for the early Voronezh poems.[6] But the occasionality also harks to other social settings, such as that in which Suleyman Stalsky, a Caucasian poet co-opted into Stalinism and satirized in one poem here, began composing.[7] Another writer from the Caucasus (and one of Stalsky's translators into Russian), Effendi Kapiyev (1909–1944), wrote:

> In the distant mountains of Dagestan, there are villages of goldsmiths, of tightrope walkers, of tinsmiths. It might seem strange, but in Dagestan there is also a village of poets. In this village, there's a singer living in practically every house. Before starting a song, your standard poet will ask the people what song he should sing: about love or hate, joy or grief? The people ask the singer for a song about love, but such that there's also hate in it; a song about hate, but such that there's also love in it; a song about grief, but such that there's also some joy in it; a song about joy, but such that there's also some grief in it, however little. The people of Dagestan, few in number, have placed these demands on their poets and singers for centuries, and they characterize a great and genuine poetry. Poems short and long are not born without pain and joy. In the mountains, the same needle sews the wedding dress as the shroud. So the poet's pen must communicate all of the heart's feelings.[8]

And of course, as the reader can conclude from the years in which they died, as stated in the respective biographical notes, many of the addressees of these poems would become those that Mandelstam had in mind in two lines from the poem that became known as 'Leningrad', which insistently invokes the city's original name:

> Petersburg, every address in my head
> will help me track down a voice from the dead.[9]

---

[6] See note 116.
[7] See note 100.
[8] Stalsky's Russian Wikipedia page.
[9] It's worth noting that besides the literati, party members, other members of the Soviet elite, and those with Tsarist or rival socialist affiliations who have loomed

II

I use the term "occasional" here for want of something better. "Light verse" implies intended publication, but only the "Fables" that close this book fall into that category. Alexander Mets's Mandelstam edition (see Translator's note) uses a designation *stikhotvoreniya "na sluchay"* that derives from Nadezhda Mandelstam's mention of such poems in her memoirs, translatable as "off-the-cuff verse" or "verse on the fly" to capture these poems' spontaneity. By "occasional" here I am not referring to the tradition of stately verse beginning with Horace's hortations to Augustus on showing an upstart Egyptian queen who was boss ("Friends, now is the time to drink"), taking a bad detour through Andrew Marvell's congratulatory tweet to Oliver Cromwell on killing Irish people ("And now the Irish are asham'd / To see themselves in one year tam'd"), and ending up more recently and trivially with another Andrew M.'s laureate rap on the 21st birthday of William Saxe-Coburg-Gotha.[10] It might be argued that Mandelstam's efforts to get on the right side of Stalin, such as "Should I take charcoal for the highest praises" also fall into this kind of occasional poetry, even if the specific circumstances of all these poems' composition clearly differ. The poems offered here are occasional on a much more down-to-earth level.

Not a few adumbrate or re-illuminate more serious poems. The theatricality of 'To a Spaniard…' has something of 'Cinema' in *Stone*. Pastiching the late medieval bandit-cum-balladeer François Villon, 'The Ballad of the Gorlin' foreshadows the homage to him in 1937's "So that the sandstone, mate of the wind". Thanking three Moscow brothers for their assistance, "I found a foothold, here in your flat" is functionally similar to, if far less complex than, the later 'Verses to Natasha Shtempel' (addressed to her but referencing the trio of Shtempel, Akhmatova and

---

large in accounts of the Purges of 1937/1938, the simple majority of this period's victims in absolute figures consisted in workers and peasants murdered by the local implementers of Stalin's meticulous instructions (denunciations certainly occurred at the grassroots level, but the killings had their own internal dynamic irrespective thereof). The historian Oleg Khlevnyuk gives the figure of 1,600,000 victims, of whom 680,000 were executed, according to official statistics (https://postnauka.ru/video/45959).

[10] Horace, *"Nunc est bibendum"* (Ode 1:37), translated by W.G. Shepherd in *The Complete Odes and Epodes* (Harmondsworth: Penguin, 1983); Andrew Marvell, 'An Horatian Ode upon Cromwell's Return from Ireland' in *The Complete Poems*, ed. Elizabeth Story Donno (London: Penguin, 1972); Andrew Motion, 'On the Record' (https://www.theguardian.com/books/2003/jun/21/andrewmotion.poetry).

Nadezhda Mandelstam). Like several poems here, "I'd so like to see you a few decades later" satirizes the Soviet translation complex, a major source of Mandelstam's income in the 1920s, in which much networking and yes-comrading was needed to obtain work. It chimes with a famous eight-liner dated to November 1933 which would not be out of stylistic place in this book, if it did not take a darker turn in its final line:

> The Tatars, the Uzbeks and Samoyeds,
> the entire Ukrainian nation,
> and even the Volga Germans are ready
> for translators to visit their words.
>
> And as we speak, by my calculation,
> some Japanese guy's on a roll,
> rendering me into perfect Turkish
> as he penetrates my soul.

Poets will not be alone in recognizing Mandelstam's frustration at having to pay the rent not from his primary vocation but from a (for him) very secondary activity, literary translation. There were and are worse ways of earning a living, of course. But there also exists a generalized suspicion of translation, especially literary translation, still virulent today, despite translators' efforts over recent years to achieve the respect and discriminatory judgment accorded other specialists.[11] Given the above poem's iteration of such hostility, this translator prefers to read it in the light of the publisher's ball's-up that started the Gornfeld Affair of 1928/9. The publisher in question mis-credited Mandelstam as the translator of the Belgian author Charles De Coster's retelling of the early 16th century tales of Till Eulenspiegel, whose existing Russian translation by Arkady Gornfeld Mandelstam had been contracted to merely revise.[12]

---

[11] The reasons for this hostility are complex. Briefly, they may in any one case involve the following. A "foreign" text can provide a target for latent xenophobia; historically, the framing of translation as subordinate to original writing has "feminized" the activity, offering an outlet for misogyny; academic specialists' gate-keeping role vis-à-vis the original is challenged; and more generally, the human urge to wag a finger given half a chance finds ideal conditions here: unsophisticated reviewers continue to figure micro-level divergence of translations from originals as *per se* wilfulness or sloppiness in order to evade the much more demanding task of assessing a translation on the macro-level.

[12] The publisher was Land and Factory. See note 83.

The ensuing hoohah in which Mandelstam was accused of plagiarism provided members of the RAPP (Russian Association of Proletarian Writers) with a useful opportunity to attack a literary and political opponent. The affair's effect on Mandelstam recalls that of the execution of his friend and poetry ally Nikolai Gumilyov in 1921 for involvement in an alleged planned coup: hardly making Mandelstam receptive to really existing Bolshevism, that event prompted his surreptitious lament for Gumilyov and realization/articulation of where things were going, "One night, as I washed in the yard".

The brief Stalin-period satires that close this book are not so different in style from the late "serious" poems rooted in the quotidian, if less humorously so, such as "What dreadful spot are we headed for now" and "What street are we on?" (in her memoirs, Nadezhda Mandelstam refers to the latter as a joke poem that made it into a proper sequence, *The Voronezh Workbooks*). And it's one step from the subversive humour of "A tailor with a decent head", written *en route* to Mandelstam's first, truncated station of internal exile in the Urals, to the subversive subjectivity of the poems he would write in the more extended period of exile in Voronezh. Besides the well-known 'Stalin Epigram' and the 'Ode to Stalin' (posthumously conferred titles), we also have in effect the Stalin Quatrain ("Relieved of all tasks when the truth was revealed"). The serious poetry's allusiveness to the literatures, languages and cultures of Biblical Judea, ancient Greece, the Roman empire, Renaissance Italy and Belle Époque France is repurposed here. The main stations of Mandelstam's life – St. Petersburg, Moscow, Voronezh – as well as the ones he hopped off and on at – Paris, the Crimea, the Caucasus – are revisited. The difficulties and absurdities of Soviet life, the effects of industrialization and collectivization, the shifts in literary climate signalled by the periodic restructuring of Soviet publishing, and the acts of solidarity and kindness appear here too. So the *Occasional and Joke Poems* are a descant to the main themes of the serious work, sometimes blending into them. Clare Cavanagh argues that seriousness and humour are intimately linked in Mandelstam's late work,[13] and in their down-to-earthness and anti-other-worldiness, these poems can likewise be viewed as being prototypically Acmeist (more on this term in IV).

The poems are also of interest for what they don't do. In contrast to the intermittent playful dialogue with Akhmatova, there's not a word on or to Marina Tsvetaeva here. On Mandelstam's side, their poetic and

---

[13] *Osip Mandelstam and the Modernist Creation of Tradition* (Princeton: Princeton University Press, 1995), pp. 220–232.

personal relationship is first embodied in four "serious" poems from 1916 (including the poem excerpted here in the note to "I found my feet back here in your flat") and continues in many further links between their work, though Mandelstam would deliver a sexist dismissal of her poetry in his 1922 essay 'Literary Moscow' and describe himself to Akhmatova as an "anti-Tsvetaevan" (in private communication and a rejoinder unpublished in her lifetime, Tsvetaeva in turn rejected some of his work). Nor is there anything recognizably to Pasternak, the dialogue with him proceeding through at least three later "serious" poems in the *New Verses*. There is certainly social and literary satire and affectionate irony directed at friends, but notwithstanding some rivalry and feuding, only rarely is there actual invective.

This is in some ways surprising. Prose pieces of Mandelstam's – such as the aforesaid 'Literary Moscow', 1923's 'An Attack' (on the Russian poetry audience, unable to keep up), and a 1913 review of Igor Severyanin – could be caustic. And in personal encounters Mandelstam could be more than forthright, physically as well: at the Moscow Poets' Café in 1918, Mandelstam tore up a wad of execution orders a Cheka officer was brandishing to show off his power, and in 1934 the poet assaulted the writer and literary functionary Alexei Tolstoy.[14] It's not as if there wasn't cause for such forthrightness in Mandelstam's literary, political and everyday milieux, with their simmering or boiling anti-Semitism. In 1920, Blok recorded in his diary his approval of a reading by Mandelstam in which, he wrote, the artist was evident and the "little yid" no longer apparent. Following the 1913 release of a Jew accused of "ritual murder", Velimir Khlebnikov delivered an anti-Jewish diatribe at the Stray Dog Café, leading to Mandelstam – abortively – challenging him to a duel.[15] And even Sergei Gorodetsky, fellow Acmeist and an enthusiastic reviewer of Mandelstam's work, lauded him for having studied Russian so hard, implying that as a Jew he was not a native speaker of Russian. The mounting criticism of Mandelstam through the 1920s would culminate in the Gornfeld Affair, referred to above.

Two reasons suggest themselves for this lack of invective in the *Occasional and Joke Poems*. One is that the impulse to this kind of poem may fundamentally have been that of the gift, whether or not the

---

[14] See note 66.

[15] Their seconds, including Mandelstam's friend the critic, writer and theorist Viktor Shklovsky (1893–1984), talked them out of it. Ralph Dutli, *Mandelstam. Eine Biographie* (Frankfurt am Main: Fischer Taschenbuch Verlag, 2005), pp. 106–108.

addressees were identical with the recipients or audience (which also explains why the Mandelstams were so untypically remiss about recording these poems: one doesn't usually keep copies of gifts). A second is that it would all have been a bit too risky, given the deep water Mandelstam was already in without exacerbating hostility through poems that tended to circulate within the village of poets and beyond, whether Mandelstam wished them to or not. When the poetically formed invective did finally come in the shape of the Stalin Epigram ("We live, but feel no land at our feet", a poem which might be viewed as extremely serious occasional verse), it led in the immediate term to interrogation and torture in the Lubyanka, in the short term to internal exile in Cherdyn in the Urals and then Voronezh in the Black Earth region, and in the mid-term (there was now no long term) to incarceration, emaciation and death in a Gulag transit camp, likely *en route* to the lethal forced-labour conditions of the Kolyma region in the Soviet Far East.

III

To date, this work has been little translated into English, not collected as a specific corpus in English translation, and has received only a modicum of attention in either Russian or Anglophone scholarship, as far as I can tell. These are three reasons why I've provided not only an extended introduction but also considerably fuller notes, in many cases involved ones, than I did for the poems in *Concert at a Railway Station*. A further one is the greater contextualization that occasional verse in any case requires. This is, of course, in tension with the immediate impact such verse would have had on its original audience, unmediated through lengthy explanations (and as Mets notes in his introduction to this section of his edition, in some cases it is no longer possible to reconstruct the circumstances in which the observation or joke would make sense). A "serious", non-occasional or by extension "permanent" poem certainly also assumes (whether the poet admits it or not) certain things about its likely or potential audience's expectations and prior knowledge, but often pretends to be written for the multiverse. By contrast, these occasional poems are openly site-specific, composed with the assumption that the prerequisite knowledge – allusions to personal qualities of a common acquaintance, a situation experienced together – is shared by a small number of people. This volume's notes also include information which strictly speaking is extraneous (especially when referring to events subsequent to the poems' composition) or downright off-topic. If these notes get somewhat picaresque, I hope they help set the macro-literary, -social and -political scenes in which these pieces existed and persisted.

Given how Mandelstam's poetry was published – or in many cases not published at the time of its writing – it is impossible to set hard and fast criteria for inclusion in the category of occasional and joke verse. Nevertheless, this book aims to bring together more or less everything Mandelstam wrote in this vein, or which has survived and not subsequently shown to be by other hands, as several poems have been. To that end, it includes the entirety of the 'Joke Poems, Occasional Poems' section in the Mets edition. It also includes that edition's entire 'Collective' section, which gathers the poems Mandelstam co-wrote with others, as the poems there seem by their nature to practically always fall into the category of occasional or joke. Here the boundaries are also blurred, because one "collective" poem ("Enamel, diamonds, plus some gold") is really Lev Gumilyov's with a dash of Mandelstam, while non-official collectivity is evident elsewhere as well: "The waters of Phlegethon lap" is a team-up with Pushkin, who had died a century previously; a couple of poems might be considered *de facto* collaborations with Akhmatova without her permission; Mandelstam's translations of poems in a French novel he was translating as a whole are effectively a collaboration as well; and talking of French novels, there's a non-collective poem about the Goncourt brothers, who wrote all their work together. Mets's 'Ascribed' section is likewise translated whole, with the exception of one very early poem that is clearly neither occasional nor humorous. Lastly, a very few of the 'Uncompleted and Lost' poem fragments are translated, where these too seem to be occasional or humorous in nature. Arguably, these and other very spur-of-the-moment pieces might have been better left to their moment, but as they are more or less otherwise unavailable in English, I have decided to lay them on the table.

In principle, I've followed the structure, sequencing and text of the Mets edition, retaining his sceptical approach to titles likely added by scribes rather than bestowed by the author, but resorting to them where they aid intelligibility and/or contextualization. Two poems Nerler includes are excluded here: one is a brief 1916 attack on Armenian epic poetry whose ascription to Mandelstam seemed just too doubtful to Mets (notwithstanding Mandelstam's later Armenophilia). The other Mets exclusion I'm grateful for as a translator is the following poem, recorded in Maria Shkapskaya's album with a note by Vsevolod Rozhdestvensky[16] to the effect (which should be evident to those without Cyrillic as well) that this is the longest rhyme in Russian poetry:

Слышен свист и вой локомобилей —
Дверь лингвиста войлоком обили.

I have, however, sacrificed Mets's scholarly differentiations for what I hope is a readable narrative by re-integrating these ascribed, collective or fragmentary pieces back into the main sequence. This also allows poems such as the Vermel cycle, that fall between these groupings in terms of the certainty of authorship, to be presented together. The distinctions are somewhat arbitrary in any case, the main sequence in fact including at least two pieces that are fragments, if more fully readable as whole poems than those in Mets's grouping of fragments. As in the Mets edition, Mandelstam's "Fables" are collected separately at the end, as their status is somewhat different: some were published or seem to have been intended for publication.

It will be obvious to readers that several of these poems have undercurrents, or swirling surface waters, in which women have their minds and bodies written about or down to in sexist and/or misogynistic ways, or their daily work or activities are laughed at, or which in at least one case (the very first poem in fact) trivialize violence against them. This applies not least to one ascribed poem ("As in the primates, there's something which you") I would hope (but have no grounds to believe) has been misattributed. Two of the Vermel poems, playing with their subject's profession as dermatological researcher, are violent and gendered fantasies that leave this translator wondering how someone who could exhibit as much empathy as Mandelstam could bring such work to mind, let alone to speech or paper. They could be seen as proof that Mandelstam had "a kind heart but a cruel mind", to reverse Emma Gerstein's attribution of "a cruel mind but a kind heart" to him. The poems to Maria Petrovykh offer a case in point, if one compares the famous "Nimble embroiderer of guilty glances"[17] with "She's sitting there with well-parched lips", printed here, though a rigidly binary distinction between "good" and "bad" poems about or to women no doubt oversimplifies matters.

I've included these poems for the sake of historical completeness, as

---

[16] See notes 72 and 53 respectively.
[17] Unpublished translation in progress as of April 2021.

regards both the *Occasional and Joke Poems* as a body of work in its own right, as well as our sense of Mandelstam's work as a whole, believing that historical poets' prejudices and disturbing figurations are better brought to light and addressed than excised from the textual base. Here too, the occasional poems parallel the serious ones, such as *Tristia*'s "I miss mosquitoes in winter" with its young-woman-as-dizzybrains trope. If nothing else, I hope the translations of these poems will be reminders of the overt assumptions and entitlements of Mandelstam's time and place (without figuring that time and place as an exotic other radically different from the assumptions and entitlements of our own), which these poems show him beholden to and replicating in this respect. These poems also show, should the court demand further proof, that the liberal humanism underpinning Mandelstam's poetry in no way precludes the expression and aestheticization of such tropes.[18] They express and expose a particular but not wholly unfamiliar culture of laughter complete with its power relations, showing who gets to laugh at who and that the freedom which laughter brings and enacts can be both in- and exclusionary.

IV

A word on the *isms* and *ists* that readers unfamiliar with Russian Silver Age poetry factions might otherwise puzzle over in the notes. By the time Mandelstam and his contemporaries appeared on the literary scene, there had already been a Golden Age of Russian poetry, driven by Alexander Pushkin, and with no disrespect to the latter, the respective precious metals reflect chronology more than the volume of actual deposits: the Silver Age of the early 20th century in fact outdid the Golden one of the early 19th century, at least in the sheer number of high-grade poets. The pre-World-War-One St. Petersburg literary intelligentsia provided a number of these, and in the great Lego kit of Modernism were hot on teaming up in mutually antagonistic playgroups (protagonists of current Anglophone poetry wars should feel at home here). Unsurprisingly, these groupings reflected – if imperfectly – both the actual models the respective poets wanted to make as well as who they liked playing with. Nuances could be made, and there were a number of other tectonic plates as well, but the basic fault-lines were as follows.

The Symbolists had established themselves in Russia around the turn of

---

[18] See note 107 for another example (Lev Gumilyov) of a suffering, dissident figure hard to squeeze into unambiguous moral rectitude.

the 19th to the 20th century as the culture's dominant style of poetry. By this time, the Russian elite no longer talked to itself in French as it had *du temps de Pouchkine*, but knowledge of the language was still widespread enough for Gallic ideas to spread with ease: Charles Baudelaire's "forest of symbols" (the pioneer plant being Edgar Allan Poe's fairly puny sapling) had been felled, harvested and bunched by Paul Verlaine and Stéphane Mallarmé, and had now reached Russia, where early adopters included Alexander Blok, Vyacheslav Ivanov and Konstantin Balmont. In more than one sense, that forest cast a lot of shadows. Max Hayward characterised (Russian) Symbolism as being "more than just a literary school or movement. It was an all-pervading climate of thought […]." He emphasizes two things. The first was the diversity of the movement, in his view united only by a desire to escape the immediate world and a sense that words were never mere referents but routes to a higher consciousness.[19] "*Va te purifier dans l'air supérieur*", Baudelaire had written, or as the young Poe had it: "All that we see and seem / Is but a dream within a dream". This was in contrast to the preceding ism, Romanticism (embodied in Russia by Pushkin), which aimed to expand access to subjectivity in the here and now: the forest it wanted to get out into was real. The second, related point that Hayward makes – echoing Gorodetsky's analysis – is that Symbolism was contradictory, not least within the work of individual poets such as Blok. The latter in fact had a good line in urban observation, which the compilers of at least one Soviet school edition lopsidedly selected at the expense of his more usual paeans to passing women he fancied. In any event, the young Mandelstam seems to have been sure why he didn't like Symbolism: the Symbolists, he wrote in an essay on Villon when he was 19, were in love with things in the way that owners are: they were proprietors of meaning.[20] In the village of poets, they were the absentee landlords.

Symbolism's later challengers included two important movements. The first was the Futurists, with their manifest(o) intent to "throw Pushkin off the Steamship of Modernity".[21] Their practice also varied widely: despite typographical appearances, Vladimir Mayakovsky wrote quite regularly structured verse (ultimately indebted to the guy the Futurists wanted to throw overboard) if with a radical expansion in vocabulary and register;

---

[19] Introduction to *Poems of Akhmatova*, co-translated with Stanley Kunitz (New York, NY: Mariner Books, 1997), pp. 6–7.
[20] For translations of Mandelstam's prose, see *The Collected Critical Prose and Letters*, translated by Jane Gary Harris and Constance Link (London: Collins Harvill, 1991, among other editions).
[21] David Burlyuk et al., 'A Slap in the Face of Public Taste', 1912.

other instantiations included the mythogeographical linguafuturity of Velimir Khlebnikov (also with his debts though: his 1920/21 'Sayan' could be straight out of Pushkin) and the *zaum* ("trans-mental") poetry of Alexei Kruchonykh, neither amenable to nor requiring translation. Not going quite as far as the Ramones in giving all the band members the same surname, some of this outfit would habitually refer to themselves by their name plus affiliation, viz. "Vladimir Mayakovsky, Futurist". In their refusal to respect the word as such, in Mandelstam's view, they were however merely repeating, if varying, the Symbolists' mistake (Nikolai Gumilyov described their relationship to Symbolism as being "hyenas following the lion"[22]). To venture a quasi-Trotskyist comparison, Mayakovsky's merry band were the Bolsheviks (with whom Mayakovsky soon aligned himself) who would usurp private ownership of meaning only to take possession of it themselves. In the village of poets, it was they who were storming the manor house.

The second group of challengers were the Acmeists, of whom Mandelstam was a member, not at the moment of the group's formation but later contributing an important manifesto, 'The Morning of Acmeism' (1912/1913, but not published until 1919). The latter set out the criticisms of the Symbolists and Futurists cited above, and built on their first articulation by Mikhail Kuzmin (not himself a card-carrying Acmeist) in 1910. In his essay 'On Beautiful Clarity' Kuzmin had referred to "unnecessary fog" (viz. the Symbolists) and "acrobatic syntax" (viz. the Futurists) in Russian poetry, and pleaded for poetry to be "logical in conception, construction and syntax" (his own banner was "Clearism"). The Acmeist attack on Symbolism was also framed in geometrical terms by Gorodetsky, perhaps under the influence of Kazimir Malevich, whose accurately titled Suprematist paintings 'Black Square' and 'Black Circle' appeared the same year:

> Approximation is a very important method in mathematics, but it is inapplicable to art. The way a square can eventually approximate a circle through the stages of the octagon and the decahexagon might be mathematical thinking, but in no sense is it *artis mente*. In art, there is only the square and the circle.[23]

---

[22] 'Symbolism's Legacy and Acmeism', 1913.
[23] 'Certain Tendencies in Contemporary Russian Poetry', 1913.

Gorodetsky and Gumilyov were the group's organizers, while other members or affiliates of varying centrality included Anna Akhmatova (its secretary, what else), Georgy Ivanov, Mikhail Lozinsky, Vladimir Shileyko, Vladimir Narbut, Irina Odoyevtseva and Nikolai Otsup. Akhmatova's later prose on Pushkin indicates that they were jumping in after him with a lifebelt. Another Acmeist metaphor was architecture, the poet designing and building their cathedral into and against the void. In village-of-poets terms, Acmeists were the honest craftspeople, preserving honourable traditions in the midst of modernization.[24]

The differences between Symbolism and Acmeism might become, so to speak, clearer from the following minimal pair of poems. Both eight-liners appear to proceed from the impulse of an evening walk. The first is by arch-Symbolist Valery Bryusov, dated 1900:

> EVENING LIGHT
>
> I love the evening when the first lamp shows,
> the sky still pale before the stars appear.
> How strangely people gaze from fading shadows.
> They look at me and need no shame or fear.
>
> Silent and sad, in thought, they pass between.
> As if their brother, I forgive their sins
> because we all slide on the brink of dreams
> and shadows hold both them and me within.

Without knowing whether Mandelstam knew this poem specifically (though it's likely – he kept close tabs on the competition), I would suggest that the following 1913 poem from *Stone* can be read as a translation of the above from Symbolism to Acmeism:

> In the quiet suburbs the porters
> are scraping away at the snow,

---

[24] My metaphors are intended to illuminate the respective poetics of these groups rather than the actual politics and origins of the practitioners. Cross-faction, nearly all were from families for whom the 19th century's agricultural, commercial or industrial proprietarianism – the term adopted by Thomas Piketty for private property's sacrosanctity – had worked out fine. Some were aristocrats, including Narbut, who was an Acmeist Bolshevik: see note 70 for how real-life manor-house-storming worked out for him.

and the bearded peasants are walking
beside me along this road.

Women gleam in their headscarves,
the crazy mongrels are yapping,
and crimson roses on samovars
sparkle in houses and taverns.

The rhyme approximations in the latter are a product of my translation process rather than flexible patterning on Mandelstam's part: Acmeism largely, though not exclusively, left the relatively regular structures of highbrow Russian poetry intact. I'll leave the reader to assess what the real difference in approach is here. Though the careful carving of Acmeism's early totems, such as Mandelstam's architectural homages, Akhmatova's dramatizations of inter-personal dilemmas, and Nikolai Gumilyov's expeditions-in-verse might suggest otherwise, the literary game was valued at the Guild of Poets, the grouping from which Acmeism emerged. With their observations of and rootedness in the everyday, these occasional poems represent one more working-out of Acmeist poetics for Mandelstam.[25]

Two final remarks on isms. The parallels between Acmeism on the one hand and Anglo-American Imagism and more generally early Anglophone Modernism on the other have been spotted before, not least in seminal Mandelstam scholarship by Clarence Brown and Clare Cavanagh (as a youthful fan of first-generation Modernism, the present translator was glad of the chance to practice being an *Imagiste* by translating his first Mandelstam poem, the one just cited, in 1995).[26] Besides some of the

---

[25] For all three groupings and many of the poets mentioned in this book, the website *ruverses.com* is a well-presented portal for translations by various hands, sometimes over-archaicized or under-Englished, but still a good place to get an overview.

[26] Clarence Brown, *Mandelstam* (Cambridge: Cambridge University Press, 1973), pp. 136–139; Cavanagh op. cit., pp. 14–28. A promising candidate for Anglophone parallels, not least in its evening setting, is T.S. Eliot's 1920 'Preludes'. From a Russian Silver Age perspective, it starts off all nice and Acmeisty: "The winter evening settles down / With smell of steaks in passageways. / Six o'clock. / The burnt-out ends of smoky days." But by the end, we're back at something not far off Symbolism: "The notion of some infinitely gentle / Infinitely suffering thing." A parallel in German poetry might be the Rilke of 'The Panther' (from 1907's *New Poems)*, rather than the regression to Symbolism in Rilke's later *Duino Elegies* and *Sonnets to Orpheus.*

respective exponents' Hellenism and the frequently urban settings, as well as the common explicit reference points of Théophile Gautier and François Villon, the most obvious intersection is the insistence on letting the image speak for itself, kick-started in Imagism's case from Ezra Pound's mediated reception of Tang Dynasty Chinese poetry and Japan's *renga / haiku* tradition. The Acmeists seem to have thought this up on their own though, or looked back again to pre-Symbolist poetry in Russia, such as Pushkin, or found their models of clarity in the French novel as Kuzmin did. Given their default setting of relatively regular structures rather than full-throated *vers libre* as in Pound's case, and notwithstanding the Symbolist tenebrosity, Acmeism's closer parallel might be the Hart Crane of poems such as 'In Shadow', which begins:

> Out in the late amber afternoon,
> Confused among chrysanthemums,
> Her parasol, a pale balloon,
> Like a waiting moon, in shadow swims.

It's also tempting to not only look for parallels in the Anglophone poetry collectives that were contemporary to the Russian groupings outlined above, but also to map these differences in poetics onto today's low-intensity poetry conflicts. Skirmishes about the notion of craft, its necessity or weaponization, spring to mind. Some of these developments, such as contemporary sound poetry's augmentation of the Futurist *zaum* tradition, or Seamus Heaney's reception of Mandelstam himself, are not only parallel to but constitutive of such differences.[27] Gorodetsky's castigation of the Symbolists, "Incomprehensibility was easier than they thought", is still worth a ponder. But such a comparison is beyond the scope of this introduction, and the blinking motorway warning here is that the comparison would need to begin (though not necessarily end) with the differences between the Russian Silver Age's poetry blocs on their own terms rather than as we project the differences of our own time onto them.

---

[27] Valeri Scherstjanoi is one prominent inheritor of the *zaum* tradition, e.g. https://www.lyrikline.org/en/poems/zahm-se-11071; Seamus Heaney, see for example 'Osip and Nadezhda Mandelstam', *London Review of Books* Vol. 3 No. 15, 20 August 1981.

V

No translator from Russian gets by without a note on the transliteration of names, and I've been particularly aware of this in preparing a book which refers to so many named individuals, a few of them familiar in the West, many more not so. In principle, I follow here a simplified version of the BGN/PCGN romanization system, sacrificing for general readability the scholarly accuracy that would enable names to be reliably reverse-engineered back into Cyrillic. Like many translators, I usually retain established transliterations, including but not limited to that of the name of Mandelstam himself, but bend the rules in some cases, preferring for example "Gumilyov" to the phonologically misleading "Gumilev" sometimes encountered. Where stress is counter-intuitive or uncertain for an English speaker, I underline the stressed vowel on the surname's first occurrence in the main note on the person in question. Except where the familiarity rule definitely applies (such as to Mandelstam), surnames of Germanic or Judeo-Germanic origin are transliterated as Russian names or re-Germanicized on a case-by-case basis, depending on whether the bearer of the surname in question appears, without exhaustive historical research, to have had a strong and very recent connection to the Teutonosphere. Some first names (such as Aleksandr) are smoothed out to their English equivalent. Patronymics (wedged between first names and surnames in Russian when a full name is given, e.g. Osip Emilevich Mandelstam) are omitted except where pertinent.

Two final preliminary clarifications for those less familiar with Russian history. The city founded by Peter the Great in the 18th century and not exactly self-deprecatingly christened St. Petersburg was renamed Petrograd at the outset of World War One when a German-sounding name for the imperial capital seemed inopportune. It retained that name until the death of Lenin in 1924, whereupon Lenin took Peter's place and the city was renamed Leningrad. The name reverted to St. Petersburg in 1991 at the end of the Soviet Union. In this introduction and the notes to the poems, I refer to the city as it was called in the respective period.

Even more confusingly than the names of imperial cities or Silver Age poetry factions, the Soviet/Russian secret police / secret service (responsible for both domestic surveillance and foreign espionage) was renamed and reorganized several times. As Hannah Arendt set out in *The Origins of Totalitarianism,* such restructuring was a prototypical example of the dynamic uncertainty of totalitarian systems, contrary to external perceptions of their monolithic immobility. Following the Revolution and during the Civil War, the organization's name was the Cheka, or Special Commission. Through the 1920s and into the 1930s it was initially the GPU and then the OGPU. In July 1934 it became the NKVD (a name that had originally referred merely to the Interior Ministry in Russia proper), not long after Mandelstam's first arrest occasioned by his poem "We live, but feel no land at our feet". Further renamings ensued in the late 1940s and early 1950s, as Stalin rebooted his redivide-and-conquer approach following the wartime lull in institutional reshuffling. After his death, as the Soviet Union reverted to stolid authoritarianism from disorienting totalitarianism, the agency's name settled into the more familiar KGB. The latter's First Directorate (that did the foreign spying) was hived off into the SVR when the Soviet Union collapsed, the remainder is now the FSB, and there also exists a military secret service called the GRU that survived the end of the Soviet Union. What exactly each of these rival agencies does in practice is not certain, a strategy that seems familiar.

Occasional and Joke Poems

To a Man Who Acted a Spaniard ("A Riddle Unravelled") [28]

Each night, this Spaniard goes
to his aunt's last rites in Zaragoza.
She lies there lifeless. He's lost her,
but never once lowers his nose.
He has a quick smoke in the crypt,
and then nips home forthwith
to his girl from Iberian parts.
"Who's this then," he asks as he grips
her hair, "this chump you're with?!
My funeral attendance is nil.
I don't even have any aunts.
It was Russian, that cig in Seville!
Now I'm here – by the beard of Gibberoza,
the moustache of Bombardoza!"

1909 (?)

If I'm honest with you, [29]
at half-past two
the alphabet's hard
on the waiting bard,
and the wise man legs it.
Now where's that exit?

14 March 1911

---

[28] *A Riddle Unravelled* was a comedy by Vladimir Trakhtenberg (1860–1914), performed in 1909 and 1917, hence the uncertainty about the poem's dating. The poem was addressed to the actor Sergei Antimonov (1880–1954) and preserved among his papers in the Russian State Archive of Literature and Art.

[29] Written at the Tower salon in St. Petersburg, run by the Symbolist poet and mystically minded polymath Vyacheslav Ivanov (1866–1949). The poem refers to a tradition of poets reading their poems in alphabetical order of their surnames. Recorded in the album of the translator and literary chronicler Friedrich Fyodorovich Fiedler (1859–1917; a.k.a. FFF, or F^3).

To be like a toy, that's what you'd change, [30]
but your clockwork is totally broken.
No soul here dares to creep within range
of your cannons without a good poem.

1911

Blok [31]
is our master,
our wizard of sin.
Shock
and disaster –
the jewels of our king.

10 December 1911

---

[30] Written by Mandelstam in the poetry album of Anna Akhmatova (1889–1966), in response to a 1911 poem of hers beginning "They're leading hobby horses down the avenue" (part of the 'At Tsarskoye Selo' cycle). Akhmatova's second stanza reads:

> Memory's strange: my spirits had fallen,
> raving as if my life were through.
> But I have become a toy and recall
> my rosy friend, the cockatoo.

[31] Alexander Blok (1880–1921) was the most prominent Russian poet of his generation. This poem is one of several by various hands gathered at the Vienna, a St. Petersburg restaurant, who had elected Blok as their "king". Recorded by Vladimir Pyast (see note 102); the poem was initially misattributed to another participant at the meal, Vasily Gippius (see note 34).

The cow is chomping its hay, [32]
a duchess is gobbling her jelly,
and the count's gone schizocelli
by half-one, around the chalet.

Around 1911

---

[32] Collectively written with Georgy Ivanov (see note 38) and Grigory Rabinovich, a friend of Mandelstam's since their teenage years (see also note 35).

Recorded in Rabinovich's memoirs, which state that this poem was one of a series the trio wrote about a count. In this poem, the count had attended a reading by the then cult poet Igor Severyanin (1887–1941), leading light of the Ego-Futurists, one of Russian Futurism's two main sub-factions. The poem parodies Severyanin's 'Dell'Acqua Torre', which begins:

> "Be off to Queen Victoria! Go!
>   Across to that foreign shore!
> Tell her the Duchess says hello,
>   the Duchess Dell'Acqua Torre.
> On that regal flower, a State has grown.
>   Go and find a chalet
> whose guard bears an aster, all his own,
>   a star where the dark holds sway.

In 1913, the journal *Hyperboria* published Mandelstam's brief review of Severyanin's book *The Thundering Goblet* (the title has also been translated as *The Cup of Thunder*). In the review, Mandelstam attacked Severyanin for "monstrous neologisms" and "foreign words with an exotic appeal". Putting the ego into Ego-Futurism, Severyanin got his own back a few years later in one stanza of a poem entitled 'Akhmatova's Verse':

> And equally heavy upon the ear
> is What's-The-Name-Of-The-Man? –
> "The Marble Midge" he's called round here –
> one Osip Mandelstam.

The nickname "The Marble Midge" was apparently thought up by Velimir Khlebnikov. Assuming, as is likely, that Mandelstam was aware of Severyanin's anti-Acmeist squib, this stanza's mocking of Mandelstam and his name might just be the seed, or at least a possible nutrient, of Mandelstam's auto-epigram of 1935 that begins "What street are we on?" (the poem's answer to that question is: "Mandelstam Street. / Damned if I know what that name means").

I'm closer to Acmeists by the Winter Palace ³³
than ones with Romantic white faces in Paris.

1912 (?)

---

³³ According to Anna Akhmatova, Mandelstam first met Nikolai Gumil<u>yo</u>v (1886–1921) in Paris. Gumilyov was Akhmatova's first husband, a leading Acmeist and to become a close friend of Mandelstam's. He was wearing a top hat and had a powdered face, like a *pierrot*, a Parisian pantomime figure. Preserved in Akhmatova's memoir *Pages from a Diary on Osip Mandelstam*.

Pastoral [34]

Germanic forests echo with horns
and the ominous knocking of faculty-peckers.
Students whose hair's no better than beggars'
hurry to harry the fabled fawns.

The grim whipper-in is *Radlov*: "Down!"
he screams at these romanticist hounds.
See how your haul of river nymphs drowns,
yes you, knight scholarly, name of *Herr Braun*!

Anichkov dams the intellectual flow
by cramming his gullet with biscuits, though.
Kogan just leaves the symposium to it:

"Your paper? I'd have to be drunk to review it!"
Romanticism's top cat around here,
and papers are what gets flushed from its rear.

15 October 1912

---

[34] Collectively written with Mikhail Lozinsky (see note 44) and Vasily Gippius (1890–1942, poet and scholar, a member of the proto-Acmeist Guild of Poets at this time, died in the siege of Leningrad).

The trio put the sonnet together at Lozinsky's flat straight after the General Meeting of the Neophilological Society at St. Petersburg University. The society was affiliated with the university's Department of Romance and Germanic languages, and both society and department were at this time headed by Professor Fyodor (Friedrich) Braun (1862–1942), who had graduated with a thesis on the Anglo-Saxon epic poem *Beowulf*. In 1920 he was to move to the University of Leipzig, working there till 1932, signing the vow of allegiance of German professors to Hitler in 1933, and remaining in the city until his death.

Ernest Radlov (1854–1928), Russian philosopher, who responded to Braun's paper at the meeting in question. Post-revolution, he edited a journal called *Thought*, which was closed down. Yevgeny Anichkov (1866–1937), literary critic and historian, expert on Shakespeare and paganism; from 1918 until the end of his life he lived largely in Belgrade. Pyotr Kogan (1872–1932), literary and linguistic scholar, at this time a lecturer in the department and an enthusiastic Marxist.

In a piece of low-level and no doubt deliberate historical irony, this poem was included in a 2008 festschrift for the Mandelstam scholar Georgy Levinton.

It's 1912, and the powers have ordained [35]
that Mustamäki must make a new saint.

Of abominable parents begotten, he is
fat-cheeked as an apple, elected to bliss.

He's pawned his silver and flogged his clothes
to pay one thousand denarii he owes.

The menials banish all ragged *sans*-jackets.
The residents eye their household assets.

As he wanders the sites of this holy land,
they shout: "Look out, there's Dandelstam!"

1912 (?), ascribed

---

[35] Published in Paris in 1931 by Georgy Ivanov in a collection of humorous verse. Also recorded in the memoirs of Mandelstam's friend Grigory Rabinovich. The latter's father ran a small hotel in Mustamäki (in Russian, Mukhino), a rural area on the Karelian isthmus, half-way from St. Petersburg to the current border with Finland. Mandelstam took refuge there after he had argued with his parents. "[F]at cheeked as an apple" is a line from a chanson by Pierre-Jean de Béranger (1780–1857).

I hear the conjugations' bells [36]
that guide me from far away,
and now my anxieties call it a day
in the humble linguist's cell.

The wailing stops. I've borne my cross.
But the question that haunts me is this:
do I need to augment the aorist
and what's the voice of *pepaidevkos*?

Late 1912–early 1913

He was automatic, polite but hard, [37]
and forgot Verlaine, who was totally bland,
then welcomed Théophile into the pantheon,
as two dynamic generations sparred.
....
Your profile could have been cut from card,
Gumilyov, for a Chinese shadowplayer's hand.

1913 (?)

---

[36] These lines were recalled by Konstantin Mochulsky (1892–1948), a fellow student of Mandelstam's in St. Petersburg who helped him cram for a Greek exam. Mets has this poem in one stanza; Mochulsky's memoir, according to Nerler, clearly refers to two.

[37] A fragment of a sonnet to Nikolai Gumilyov, according to Sergei Rudakov (see note 116), who included it in a letter to his wife in 1935. It reappeared in the memoirs of Emma Gerstein (see note 112), who dates it 1915.

In his essay 'Symbolism's Legacy and Acmeism', published the same year as Mets putatively dates this poem, Gumilyov had cited the 19th century French poet Théophile Gautier (as well as Shakespeare, Rabelais and Villon) as a precursor of Acmeism. The description of Gautier's younger contemporary Paul Verlaine as "totally bland" is likely Mandelstam relaying Gumilyov's view rather than stating his own: in a 1910 essay on Villon, Mandelstam had seen Verlaine as "smashing the hothouses of Symbolism".

Don't look glum, [38]
just plonk your bum
on this tram that's so empty,
so number twenty.

1913 (?)

God, what a squeak! It's so bad it [39]
hurts the length of my ear.
Monsieur Critique is here...
Any "bushy pines" have had it.

Between 1910 and 1914

---

[38] Recalled by Georgy Ivanov (1894–1958, sometime Ego-Futurist turned Acmeist, emigré to France) in his memoir *Petersburg Winters*, attacked by Nadezhda Mandelstam, Anna Akhmatova and Vladimir Nabokov for inventing facts.

[39] The critic Nikolai Nedobrovo (1882–1919; the surname means "Unkind") once wrote about Akhmatova, and would often refer to a poem by Afanasy Fet (1820–1892) from the late 1860s that begins:

> The storm has made the pine-tree's bushy branches fray,
> the Autumn night has ceased the icy tears it cries,
> no lights on earth, no stars across the widowed sky,
> the wind would rip, the downpour wash it all away.

With an explanation to this effect by Vladimir Pyast, the poem was recorded in the album of Maria Shkapskaya (see note 72).

Chumpties [40]

I

Umpteen lilacs sprout:
the flowers are a-hum, paunched beetles
crawl onto a stump and pig out.
A goddess slumps in the heat.

II

Grumpy passengers pilfer
the train-guard's lumpen melons.
"Humpf! You bizzard of felons!
I'll dump you in the next river!"

1914 (?)

---

[40] *Chumpties*: in the original, 'Zhory', a nonsense genre devised by Vladimir Shileyko (1891–1930), a poet and scholar in Middle Eastern studies whose academic interests also exerted an influence on Mandelstam, and who was married to Akhmatova from 1918 to 1921. Shileyko's permission was "officially" required prior to composition, despite the fact that Mandelstam's was the first actual instance of the genre. In the case of Georgy Ivanov, Shileyko demanded the prior written consent of the poet's parents. When Ivanov told him that his father was dead, Shileyko refused permission on the grounds that the death of Ivanov's father "does not concern me".

Like so many of the literary legends and anecdotes of the time, the genre was born in the Stray Dog Café, pre-WW1 hangout of the St. Petersburg literary intelligentsia and their comfortably walleted audience. Poem preserved in Mikhail Lozinsky's archive.

An Anthology of Ancient Nonsense [41]

1 Jealousy

"Lesbia! Where have you been?" "In the arms of Morpheus." [42]
"Don't lie to me, woman! I was in them myself!"

2
The wind rips yellow leaves off the tops of the trees.
Lesbia! Over here! Look at all these fig-leaves!

3
Phoebus? Gone for a spin in his golden chariot. [43]
But he's due back tomorrow, by just the same route.

4
The taps drown out the raucous voices, but you're the host…
"Oi! Run a bath if you want, not away from your guests!"

5
Stingy Lozinskius jealously guarded his bowls [44]
and seldom dispensed a beaker of foaming wine.

---

[41] Some of these pseudo-classical verses were first presented by Mandelstam at the Stray Dog Café as translations of an unknown ancient poet called Caius Stultitius, and later published in a journal under the pseudonym Ank Sulpitsius, and still later in a handwritten book. Though first believed to constitute a collective work, they are now thought to all be by Mandelstam.

[42] *Lesbia*: muse of the Roman poet Catullus (c.84–c.54 B.C.E). *Morpheus*: Greek god of dreams.

[43] *Phoebus*: literally "bright" in Greek, another name for Apollo, god of the sun.

[44] Mikhail Lozinsky (1886–1955): close early collaborator of Mandelstam's, a fellow member of the Guild of Poets from which the Acmeists emerged, and later a noted translator of Dante. The journal *Hyperboria* was an important forum for many poets in the pre-WW1 years, and its editorial meetings took place in Lozinsky's flat from 1911 to 1914. Lozinsky was in fact known for his generosity (this is the joke), later providing material assistance to Mandelstam during the latter's internal exile in Voronezh. Two days after Nikolai Gumilyov's arrest in 1921, Lozinsky was questioned by the Cheka because of his Acmeist connection. He nevertheless survived the 1938 "Translators' Case" in which Benedikt Livshits and David Vygodsky (see notes 60 and 79 respectively) were to perish.

Dining with neophytes, once he'd reclined, he told them:
"The Scythians used to love wine. I love my friends."

6
When stingy Lozinskius saw off his guests,
he'd seldom pop roubles into their mitts.
When less ambitious ones asked for just kopecks,
he'd cough up his funds right there in triumph.

7
"Mortal, from whence hast thou come?" "Shileyko's. [45]
His place is amazing! You think you're seeing things.
He sits in deep armchairs, takes goose for tea.
You touch this button and lights light up by themselves."
"Traveller, if such reside upon the Fourth Ring Road,
what gods are those whom we might find on the Eighth?"

8
"I love you!" he screamed for the thousandth time, and was done.
No doubt we'll hear him make it one thousand and one.

9
Tightly embraced, the couple glimpsed a huge star
that was only the moon, discussions revealed in the morning.

1911–1914

---

[45] Vladimir Shileyko: see note 40.

Baron Emil grabs a knife: [46]
that damn pic's not true to life!
But Baron Emil, you've lost this one.
Baron Emil, the portrait's gone.

1914

To improve her hair strength, one lady [47]
once rubbed her scalp with kerosene
while up and about in her nightie.
What happened? The kerosene made
her hair a jungle not seen
since the Eocene, dense and mighty.

1914 (?)

---

[46] Emil Mandelstam, the poet's father, threatened to tear to pieces the first portrait done of Mandelstam, by the artist Anna Zelmanova (1891–1952; one of many objects of Mandelstam's infatuation). Recalled by a certain V.S. Sreznevsky.

[47] Poem recorded by S.G. Vysheslavtsev (1890–1975), who heard Mandelstam deliver several extempore poems during meals in the course of a winter stay at a small hotel in Kuokkala (now Repino) near St. Petersburg. None of the other extempore poems have survived.

That is Altmann. He is painter. [48]
He is now an old, old man.
Altmann is a German name.
German. Means an old, old man.

Old school. That is Altmanns art.
Always work so hard how he can.
He is sad he work so hard.
Make him now an old, old man.

1915 (?)

There's a milk on which Pallas and I both feed: [49]
she might be a heathen, but milk's what I need!

15 August 1917

---

[48] Natan Altman (1889–1970, "Altmann" if relexicalized back to German) painted a famous portrait of Anna Akhmatova. According to the poet, critic and Guild of Poets participant Georgy Adamovich (1892–1972), Mandelstam used to read this poem in a German accent. Published in 1924 in the Paris-based emigré journal *Zveno* (The Link), as part of a feature by Georgy Ivanov.

[49] The original Pallas was the Greek goddess Athena's foster-sister (in Russian, literally "milk-sister"). This couplet arose from an encounter with the poet and salon-organizer Pallada Bogdanova-Belskaya (1885–1968), whose supposed notoriety began when two rejected admirers of hers (allegedly) shot themselves, and continued through four marriages. Igor Severyanin, Georgy Ivanov and several other poets addressed pieces to her.

In the Crimean town of Alushta, she and Mandelstam bought milk from the same cow-owner, Mandelstam recording the poem in her album, which was well-known in literary circles of the time. Nerler gives a first line that literally means "I'm fed by the milk of Pallas the Classical", from a different source, the musician and bibliophile Moses Lesman (1902–1985).

One morning, Sergeant Stutter ⁵⁰
popped round to his great-grandmother (…)

1910s (?)

You're breathing into my trumpet, young man! ⁵¹
Imagine you're six feet under, young man!

Late 1919–early 1920

Yes it was twenty thousand I owed you! ⁵²
It could have been thirty, so quit moaning.

Late 1920–early 1921

---

⁵⁰ Fragment recorded by Nadezhda Mandelstam and preserved in the archive of Pavel Luknitsky (see note 65).
⁵¹ Recorded in the memoirs of Ilya Ehrenburg (1891–1967, Soviet writer) and recited by Mandelstam in the Crimean town of Feodosia, near Koktebel where the Mandelstams and many literati spent summers at the home of the hospitable poet-cum-visionary and translator Maximilian Voloshin (1877–1932). Nerler gives the poem a title, "Ghazal" (the couplet's use of repeated end words recalls the Arabic form of the ghazal).
⁵² Mandelstam apparently wrote this in the album of Roza Rur, who ran a small shop on the premises of the publishers World Literature (*Vsemirnaya literatura*), and then immediately tore it out again. The Nerler edition includes a dedication to "Roza the black marketeer". Like "That is Altmann. He is painter", published in 1924 in the Paris-based emigré journal *Zveno* (The Link), as part of a feature by Georgy Ivanov.

Pushkin got given an avenue. Fiery old Lermontov too. [53]
How revered you are, Mr. Christmas, with your ten roads,
and that's just in your own lifetime!

Spring 1921 (?), ascribed

---

[53] Mikhail Lermontov (1814–1841), Russia's most famous 19th century poet after Pushkin, though best known outside of Russia for his formally innovative short novel *A Hero of Our Time*. Vsevolod Rozhdestvensky (1895–1977; his surname means "Christmas"), poet, attended the meetings of the Third Guild of Poets in Petrograd's House of the Arts (see next note). He would indeed go on to enjoy a decorated literary career; the German Slavist Wolfgang Kasack described him as "a conformist, though not a writer of propaganda". As well as a *Rozhdestvenskaya ulitsa* in Moscow, there are roads of the same name in a number of major and minor cities in Russia and Ukraine. Poem preserved in Maria Shkapskaya's album.

The Fallen Officer (A Ballad) [54]

Dedicated to the poet N. Otsup

The Colonel's eggs
passed inspeggtion.

He ate his colleggtion
without eggception.

Let us mourn this Colonel
who fell in eggtion.

1920 or 1921

---

[54] Nikolai Otsup (1894–1958) had a poem including the lines "And he lies with his arms crossed, / the fallen officer." He was apparently reciting this poem at the Union of Poets, at a reading where rationed (and by now rotten) eggs were being distributed, one per person. A certain Colonel Belavenets, of advanced years, who had already received his solitary egg, interjected "What do you all want a single egg for? Give them to me, I'm already getting quite a collection."

This information is from Irina Odoyevtseva (1895–1990), born Iraīda Heinike in Riga, Acmeist poet, novelist and later a prominent memoirist, Nikolai Gumilyov's favourite student, and Georgy Ivanov's wife. The poem was collectively written by Mandelstam, Gumilyov and Ivanov. It was included in a 1930 novel by Olga Forsh (1873–1961) whose title has been translated as *The Lunatic Ship*: the novel was set in the House of the Arts in Petrograd, which housed writers and poets including Alexander Blok and Yevgeny Zamyatin (author of the early dystopian novel *We*).

Otsup co-organized the Guild of Poets with Gumilyov and Mikhail Lozinsky. He emigrated in 1921 after both his brother and Gumilyov had been shot by the Bolsheviks. Later married to the Polish actor, director and producer Diana Karenne (1888–1940, or according to some reports, –1968). Later still, he was a French soldier, German prisoner-of-war and Italian partisan.

Archangel Michael passed straight through [55]
the altar screen with its golden icons.
In the quiet of night, he sniffed Valerian
and fired off his questions:
"What use is plaited hair to you,
or satin over your gleaming shoulders"
(...)

1921

(...) Kandelaki's aide, Brekhnichov by name, [56]
who took the place of a dog on a chain

1921

---

[55] Fragment recalled by Anna Akhmatova in her memoir *Pages from a Diary on Osip Mandelstam*. According to her, the poem was a parody of Anna Radlova (1891–1949), poet, salon-organizer and Shakespeare translator. Accused of Nazi collaboration (likely through having ended up outside the Soviet Union's borders when the war finished), Radlova was sentenced to ten years in the Gulag, where she died of a stroke. She had an admirer called Valerian Chudovsky (1882–1937 or possibly 1938, shot), a literary critic described by Rozhdestvensky as a "red-haired peacock". Valerian itself is a soporific herb.

[56] Fragment recalled by Nadezhda Mandelstam from the Mandelstams' stay in Georgia towards the end of the Russian Civil War. David Kandelaki (1896–1938, shot), at the time of the poem Commissar for Education in Georgia, later a diplomat who carried out secret talks with Hitler. Iona Brikhnichov (1879–1968; the original poem slightly misspells the surname) also worked in the Education Commission; according to Nadezhda Mandelstam, a defrocked priest and apparently therefore prevented from having direct jurisdiction over priests. Kandelaki (a Georgian), she related, had issued minor translation contracts that helped out some Russian emigrants to Georgia (independent from 1917 to 1921), but was later overridden by Brikhnichov, a Russian.

The fragment appears to satirize what seems to have already been the relationship between non-Russians and Russians in the Soviet Republics at this early stage, and which would remain in place until those republics (re)gained independence in 1991: formally, local non-Russians held the top positions, but their Russian deputies had a *de facto* veto over their decisions.

So many crafts a man might practise, [57]
and money's the trough the ox finds attractive.
In Pakhom the Farmer's tax-dodging scheme,
he's taxed by a girl he hires for his harem.

1922 or 1923

---

[57] Published in the literary journal *Novy Mir* in 1978, in an article by Valentin Katayev (1897–1986). Together with Katayev, Mandelstam had been commissioned by Nadezhda Krupskaya (in charge of adult education at the time, and Lenin's wife) to write a poem unmasking the kulaks (rich farmers). Allegedly, they were getting round agricultural tax by pretending hired labourers were their family members. According to Katayev, Mandelstam castigated him when Katayev suggested an opening line in trochaic tetrameter, which according to Mandelstam had, unforgivably, no basis in the satiric tradition. This poem was Mandelstam's effort.

Pakhom: main character in Lev Tolstoy's short story, 'How Much Land Does a Man Need?', whose acquisitiveness leads him into a Faustian land deal.

Katayev was the brother of Yevgeny Petrov, one half of Ilf and Petrov, co-authors of the famous 1928 satirical novel *The Twelve Chairs* (see also note 129). In Katayev's article, Mandelstam is referred to as The Nutcracker.

[From Dmitri Shepelenko's notebooks] [58]

Poets just don't give a shit!
Just look what Dmitri's writ –
that Aglaida and her St. Bonnyface[59]
copped off but didn't embrace.

*

No silk for us but only wool –
what a miserable tribe we are!
Hellish words keep our notebooks full.
Life sweats along, but doesn't get far.

*

Your heart is alive as such,
nor is your head berefter
of talent then Melantyevna,
off cleaning. But that's not much.

8 November 1923, all three poems ascribed

---

[58] Dmitri Shepelenko (1897–1972), Russian poet, member of the Tbilisi Guild of Poets, and Mandelstam's neighbour in the Herzen House, Moscow, from 1922 to 1924, who recorded these poems.

[59] *St. Bonnyface*: Not the English St. Boniface, but Boniface of Tarsus, a slave martyred as a Christian in the southern Anatolian city in 307 having gone there to fetch relics for his owner and lover Aglaida. His body was returned to her in Rome, having as it were fulfilled its mission, and Aglaida too converted to Christianity. In the Russian folk-Orthodox tradition, Boniface is prayed to for deliverance from drunkenness. Shepelenko added the story to his notebook, and this poem was Mandelstam's reaction to the note.

As a teen, I minded the stripes of my modest mattress, [60]
the factory resin secreting its strange instalments.
Yes, the time has arrived to purchase a counterpane.
Ask Livshits why, the guy's been married twice.

1924 (?)

Aphorisms on the Nonsense of Life [61]

1

What Joseph would jot off another epigram?
A Joseph none other than Osip Mandelstam. [62]

2

At the House of the Arts, we have someone to say which
hours to take baths: that's Madame Khodasevich. [63]

---

[60] Addressed to Zinovy Davydov, just married, right-hand man of Alexander Gorlin (see note 69) at *Gosizdat*, according to Nerler. Benedikt Livshits (1886–1938), poet and translator, affiliation-wise a Futurist but close friends with Mandelstam; like David Vygodsky, arrested and executed in the "Translators' Case" (see note 79). Poem preserved in Maria Shkapskaya's album.

[61] The title parodies the German philosopher Arthur Schopenhauer's *Aphorisms on the Wisdom of Life*. These couplets mostly arose in the course of the Mandelstams' residence at the House of the Arts in Petrograd in 1920–1921 (residence at that time meaning less having the space to write and more having somewhere to live). They were preserved in the archive of Pavel Luknitsky (see note 65).

[62] "Osip" is the Russianized form of Joseph (see also note 105).

[63] Anna Khodasevich (1887–1964), then wife of the poet Vladislav Khodasevich.

3

"Edgar Khodasevich?" "Grentsion. I am he."
There's a Chénier elegy though on Alcyone… [64]

4

Meet P.N. Luknitsky, biography's *doyen*.
Milyukov? The historian? Sorry. Wrong P.N. [65]

---

[64] Edgar Grentsion (later an actor under the stage name Edgar Garrik) was Anna Khodasevich's son by her previous marriage and retained his surname when she remarried. Alycone is one of the Pleiades or one of six different mythological figures. In combination with the reference to the Franco-Greco-Levantine poet André Chénier (1762–1794), the epigram appears to refer to the mythological sacred birds of the same name (identified variously with gulls, swans or kingfishers) with which Chénier's Elegy XX begins:

Pleurez, doux alcyons! ô vous, oiseaux sacrés,
Oiseaux chers à Thétis, doux alcyons, pleurez!

In the elegy, a young bride from the Italian province of Taranto is standing at the bow of a ship taking her to meet her bridegroom when she clumsily falls into the sea upon an inopportune gust of wind and drowns. Her body is rescued by the sea-nymph Thétis for due burial, including diverse nymphs bewailing the waste of a good dress.

The exact link between the various elements in the poem are unclear to both Mets and this translator. There may be a reference to the small press Alycone, active from 1910 to 1923, which published Vladislav Khodasevich's *A Happy Little Home,* as well as work by Lozinsky and Marietta Shaginyan (see note 91).
[65] Pavel Nikolayevich Luknitsky (1900–1973), Nikolai Gumilyov's biographer and Lev Gumilyov's teacher; he later wrote a memoir of Akhmatova. Undertook expeditions to the Pamirs, where he was once taken hostage by locals and discovered Mayakovsky Peak. There's also a Pamir named after Luknitsky himself. Pavel Nikolayevich Milyuk*o*v (1856–1943), famous historian and member of the Provisional Government between the February and October Revolutions of 1917.

5

Comrade Peshkov, *be bitter*'s your maxim.
It's odd that you don't live up to that, Maxim. ⁶⁶

6

"This coal, it is peat!" It's true, your lament of course.
But Madam, not everyone calls herself Benckendorff. ⁶⁷

1920–1921; 1925 (?)

---

⁶⁶ Alexei Maximovich Peshk<u>o</u>v was the birth name of the Russian writer Maxim Gorky (1868–1936), whose pen-surname means "bitter". Critical of the Bolsheviks in the 1920s, Gorky returned to the Soviet Union in 1928.
  Gorky was to play a role in Mandelstam's arrest in 1934. This was precipitated in early May of that year when Mandelstam publicly hit the writer and literary functionary Alexei Tolstoy: the OGPU likely already knew of Mandelstam's anti-Stalin poem "We live, but feel no land at our feet", but this event seems to have set the arrest machinery in motion. Two years previously, Tolstoy had adjudicated a hearing on an incident at the Herzen House in Moscow, where the Mandelstams were living, in which Nadezhda had been hit by the writer Sergei Borodin (1902–1974, "Amir Sargidzhan" was his pseudonym) in a dispute over an unpaid debt of Borodin's. Tolstoy reprimanded Borodin but also Mandelstam. Following Mandelstam's physical reprisal, Tolstoy complained to Gorky, then President of the Union of Soviet Writers, who allegedly (and anti-Semitically, by the looks of it) said "We will teach him [Mandelstam] what happens if you hit a Russian writer".
⁶⁷ Maria Benckendorff (1892–1974), later known in the West as Moura Budberg, was at this time Gorky's lover and secretary, having previously been involved with the British spy Robert Lockhart and herself later suspected of being a double agent for the OGPU and MI5. She emigrated in January 1921, became the lover of H.G. Wells and was the great-great-aunt of British politician Nick Clegg. Alexander von Benckendorff (c. 1782–1844) had been the first head of the Tsar's secret service; Maria Benckendorff acquired her surname through marriage.

[Translations from Jules Romains's novel *Les Copains*] [68]

[1]
O water, passing through the crystalline pissoir,
your manly stream reminds me of Ambert,
from where I saw the sun above Issoire,
as it rose like a globule of Camembert.

[2]
A chestnut's awning tops the languid pissoir,
the blush of Autumn draped across Ambert:
the verdure's harmony soughs across Issoire,
to which the heart adheres like tender Camembert.

[3]
Lightning glints on the walls of Issoire,
the plains a-shimmer with plagues of Camembert!
You, the devourer of night, o Ambert,
its lunatic blacksmiths at glowing pissoirs!

[4]
O years! O hours! O burden of Issoire!
The current in the vortex filling the pissoir!
The flush of life requires that lily: hey Ambert!
Your coat-of-arms – who plaited in the Camembert?

---

[68] *Les Copains* (literally 'The Pals', translated into English as *The Boys in the Back Room* in 1937 by Jacques LeClercq) is a 1913 novel by the French writer Jules Romains (1885–1972) about the alcohol-fuelled adventures of a group of students. Mandelstam translated it into Russian, including these poems, written for the most part in *bouts-rimés* or "rhymed ends", a prescribed set of rhyme words. Ambert, famous for its cheese, and Issoire are towns in the Auvergne region. The Mandelstam Society's four-volume edition of Mandelstam's work (1993–1999) includes several more verse sections from his translation of the novel; the English translation here follows the selection in the Mets edition.

[5]
The chilly wind within the anterooms of pissoirs
is spilling quietness all over Issoire.
Gendarmes collapse at the odour of Camembert.
"I need air!"
      "I'm done for!"
            "*Incroyable!*" "Ambert!"

[6]
I hate this place and its frigging Camembert
teeming with maggots! Screw you, Ambert!
We see Issoire's rebuke to us though everywhere:
protected from looks, the ironclad pissoir.

[7]
It's very civic-minded, it is, Ambert,
with its urns *de la République*, its gleaming pissoirs.
But should we need to touch upon Issoire,
fail not to mention its stench of Camembert!

[8]
As if upon the wing, on Wednesday's dewy morn,
peregrinating by wheel, you shall, my friend high-born,
proceed towards the heights to which desire strains,
and where, like cannons firing across surrounding plains,
a morning milkman likes to thump unloaded tins.
For having downed my coffee, I shall then begin,
along the muffled roads, to propel my means of motion,
and meet upon the way an old man of great devotion,
his bristling broom – the armament that Neptune swung –
nourished in these deserted streets by equine dung.
Brimming with thoughts, o thither shall I ride the path
that leads me to the verdant Square of Arts and Crafts,
and consolation for my life that shells have notched – the smile
that warms me as it gleams from that heroic profile.
Civility's rubbish. Trivial words! Enough of them!
Till Wednesday, *n'oublie pas*! The square at five a.m.

1924 or 1925

The Ballad of the Gorlin [69]

Absalom, Ionov and *Gosizdat*
required the total surrender
of Korelenko's kingdom that
was rife with literary degenerates:
"We won't take an ounce of silvery flakes
from the mint, or Soviet tenners.
Kerenskies? They're not legal tender!
The Gorlin's all that we take!

No house can house two Alexanders.
Which one will fall on all fours?
Which one of this duo of dual commanders
will blondes and brunettes love more?
And another call that I won't make:

---

[69] Mandelstam co-wrote this with Benedikt Livshits, and the poem was preserved by Kornei Chukovsky (1882–1969), a popular children's poet in the Soviet Union.

For translation contracts, both Mandelstam and Livshits were dependent on Alexander Gorlin (1878–1938, died in detention), chief editor of the foreign languages section at the publishing house *Gosizdat*. Chukovsky called him a third-rate translator, while Mandelstam praised Gorlin's translation skills effusively in a 1929 letter to Ionov (see below), though this may have been part of strategic customer acquisition.

Two Alexanders: the second Alexander is Alexander Tikhonov (1880–1956), who ran World Literature ("Korelenko's kingdom"), which had been instructed to merge with *Gosizdat*. *Korolenko*: possibly Vladimir Korolenko (1856–1921), poet and journalist; Nerler understands his naming as a reference to Russian realist prose. And there's a third Alexander in the poem, Alexander Kerensky (1881–1970): between the February and October Revolutions in 1917, he led Russia's provisional government, which issued its own banknotes.

At the time, Ilia Ionov (1887–1942) was the head of *Gosizdat*, where he took a hard political line on publishing decisions. He later replaced Vladimir Narbut (see next note) as editor at Land and Factory. Gorky wrote a letter to Stalin in 1932 criticizing Ionov. Having served a term in a Tsarist prison and been exiled to Siberia before the First World War, he was arrested in 1937 and died in a camp in the Kolyma region in the Soviet Far East.

In the Second Book of Samuel, Absalom fatally rebels against his father, King David.

who will the walls be gazing at,
dragged in alive to *Gosizdat*?
The Gorlin's all that we take!

Patriotic Viennese ladies are proud
of their coffee's cathartic effects?
No pretty face puts chow in your mouth,
nor do tsars of global *belles lettres!*
You've soup with croutons, we've got steak,
but why keep picking nits?
Who cares what floor it is where you sit!
The Gorlin's all that we take!

Envoi:
Prince of *Gosizdat*! Oh by his lunch break
the accountant has sung like a nightingale:
"Who's after advances before any sales?
The Gorlin's all that we take!"

25 December 1924

The Party let Publius in as a youth, to its golden ranks. [70]
By the time they'd kicked him out – alas! – he was old and a wreck.

1925 (?)

---

[70] In two senses, *Publius* was a common name among Romans, thought to be etymologically related to "people" and "public". It was believed that the poem refers to Vladimir Narbut (1888–1938), Mandelstam's fellow Acmeist, turned Bolshevik, expelled from the Party in 1928, but this conflicts with the date of 1925 that Mandelstam himself had added to the manuscript. Notwithstanding poems addressed to the October Revolution and the Cheka, Narbut seems to this translator to be tonally closest to Mandelstam among the Acmeists, with a comparable proportion of idiomaticity and idiosyncrasy in his work.

The Ukrainian village he was born in bore Narbut's originally Lithuanian surname. His family appear to have been not short of a few bob: in 1912 he was able to evade a lawsuit connected to a scandalous publication by going on a five-month ethnographic expedition to Somalia and Abyssinia with Nikolai Gumilyov. During the Civil War, a Red Army unit stormed his family estate, killing his brother and wounding Narbut, whose hand had to be amputated; when the unit found out that Narbut was a Bolshevik, they visited him in hospital to say sorry. Later interrogated by White forces, he signed a statement confessing to and denouncing his own involvement with the Bolsheviks. The statement was to resurface and form the basis of Narbut's expulsion from the Communist Party, and in 1936 he was accused of Ukrainian bourgeois nationalism. While already serving his sentence in the Kolyma region, he was caught up in a new round of the Purges involving prisoners in camps. Nadezhda Mandelstam's memoirs relayed a report that he had been in a group of prisoners murdered by sinking their barge in the sea off Magadan in 1944. As regards Narbut himself, this was later disproven (it's not apparent from sources consulted whether the sinking itself actually took place). The truth, however, was brutal enough: he was shot in the camp on his 50th birthday.

Recorded by the Futurist and *zaum* ("trans-mental") poet Alexei Kruchonykh (1886–1968), with a note that this was from 'An Anthology of Ancient Nonsense' (see note 41).

You may not have known this before: [71]
two brothers in France are called Edmond and Jules de Goncourt.
If they hadn't been born and written as one, though two,
the French wouldn't prize them the way that they do.

Two brothers, one head.
Top hats and frock coats in duet.
....
For Jules has only to sketch out a tale
and Edmond stops eating, goes pale.
....
One labours to make their novel still greater,
as the other whirls round an ice cream maker.

However it's bucketing down, it's proper
to put in an evening down the Grand Opera.
Whose paragraphs made more profits or losses?
Who cares. They pass each other their galoshes.

There isn't a spot in the city, not nowhere,
they won't turn into a première,
a concert party, a *salon*.
"One recently lunched with Flaubert.
Say what you will, *mon frère*,
but *Bovary*'s coming on."

1925 (?)

---

[71] The Goncourt brothers (Edmond, 1822–1896, and Jules, 1830–1870) co-wrote all their work, and gave their name to France's Goncourt Prize.
 Fragments, also recorded by Alexei Kruchonykh (see preceding note), with additions by Pavel Luknitsky.

The fact that Maria's that gullible should have been clear to me: [72]
if you do a Brousson on Pyast, fleet-slippered as France, he'll flee.

1925 (?)

---

[72] For five years, Jean-Jacques Brousson (1878–1958) was the secretary of the novelist Anatole France (1844–1924) until fired *en route* to Argentina. In the year of France's death, Brousson published a memoir of his former employer entitled *Anatole France en pantoufles*.

Maria Shkapskaya (1891–1952), poet whose work included overtly feminist concerns; when her poetry started attracting political criticism in the 1920s for its religious inflections, she turned increasingly to journalism, including work on industrial history and later on the Nazi occupation; had a subsidiary interest in poodle-breeding, apparently. Stories by Vladimir Pyast were the source of several notes in her album, where this poem was recorded. A 1922 poem of hers (line 7 a possible echo of Mandelstam's 1921 poem "One night, as I washed in the yard") reads:

> Golgotha for women: again
> you fill your child with your strength,
> the child that you feed with yourself,
> getting no breaks, getting no breath.
>
> Until you collapse, parched, on the street,
> those who'd arrive will gnaw you inside.
> The rules of the earth are simple and strict:
> see the birth through and die.

Sonnet [73]

It's literary Sabbath at Number 9
Moss Road for a clan from the marsh. Their bash
has Gomel as Rome, the pope's Sholem Asch,
and the curly side-locks there are all canine.

The tabernacle built by that dwarfish pair
from newspapers – oh equilibrious miracle! –
matches the rabbis' cloths for the ritual,
those mattings of Spanish-Belorussian hair.

Two-foot tall with a beard, what is *that*!
A Hebrew character shaped like a hook,
David Vygodsky frequents *Gosizdat*,

his kid brother too. Facing barbarous shavers,
dwarfier still, that chief trader in books
likewise denounces the use of a razor.

1926 or 1927

---

[73] David Vygodsky (see note 79) grew up in Gomel, the second largest city in what is now Belarus. A polylingual translator, he came to specialize in Hispanic literature and worked at the publishers *Gosizdat*.

Sholem Asch (1880–1957): Polish-Jewish novelist and dramatist who wrote in Yiddish; some of his work faced obscenity charges and religious backlash in the U.S., where he lived for long periods while continuing to travel extensively to Palestine, the Soviet Union and elsewhere. Possibly translated into Russian by Vygodsky (under a pseudonymous abbreviation, and the poem hints at this).

Collectively written with Benedikt Livshits and recorded in Kornei Chukovsky's handwritten almanac.

Who's Mayakovsky's nemesis, [74]
plenipotentiary representative
of Lahūtī (that satrap once of Persia)?
O Lord, I do beseech forgiveness:
it's Shengeli, that soul from Kerch
who is the Russian iamb's shrewd observer.

Around 1927

---

[74] Abolqāsem Lahūtī (1887–1957), Persian poet and socialist, from 1922 in exile in the Soviet Union. His poems were translated into Russian by Georgy Shengeli (1894–1956), whose works also included a pamphlet attacking Mayakovsky, a study of Russian prosody, and a parody of Mandelstam's early classicism. He was later one of those to whom Mandelstam read his poem "We live, but feel no land at our feet", which became known as the Stalin Epigram. Kerch is a town in the far east of the Crimea, where Shengeli went to school. Recorded by Nadezhda Mandelstam in an undated note.

I found my feet back here in your flat: [75]
that bedside manner you three displayed,
it raised me from the dead.
And long may this sad sickly rat
remain indebted for your first aid,
which shouldn't be left unsaid.

May 1927

---

[75] Addressed to the Gornung brothers, Boris (1899–1976), Lev (1902–1993) and Yuri, the first two of whom were poets, translators and critics. In a memoir published by the Mandelstam Society in 2000, Boris Gornung related the background to this poem.

Mandelstam and Boris Gornung were repairing to the latter's flat following an abortive meeting with Vladimir Narbut, who held a post in publishing at the time. The meeting had concerned the publication of abridged translations of Western classics, in which Mandelstam and Benedikt Livshits were involved. *En route*, Mandelstam proposed that he and Gornung shin up and follow the broken wall of Moscow's Chinatown to a bridge across the Moscow river. Gornung tried to dissuade him, concerned they would get arrested. Undeterred, Mandelstam insisted they take this route, but then complained of having caught a chill. He was revived at the Gornungs' flat with aspirin, hot tea and an unspecified alcoholic drink. As a farewell and thank-you, he wrote and read them the poem above.

The poem was the culmination of an exchange over the course of the walk. Mandelstam had begun by quoting four lines of Boris Gornung's from memory:

> The house goblins scurry along the walls
> where fir trees grow from the crevices.
> Evening scowls. The churches waiting
> for the blurred but fiery ball…

Parodying four lines from an uncollected 1916 poem by Mandelstam about Moscow's Cathedral of the Assumption –

> And from the wall archangels fortified
> I viewed the city from a height quite curious.
> And Russian-named, grief gnawed at me, inside
> that walled Acropolis, that grief was glorious.

– Gornung responded:

But I love your streaks of grey, [76]
so post-and-telegraph, Sergei. (…)

1920s

    And from the wall the Moscow Soviet demolished,
    we saw the city from a lowish height.
    In the Soviet wind, we almost lost our foothold,
    and through the gaps in that cage we climbed.

Gornung later worked in Soviet publishing while privately researching Ancient Greek and Indo-European. This research remained wholly unpublished until 1950 owing to the dominance of Marrism, a theory which began by connecting some Caucasian languages to Semitic languages and ended by postulating a common Ur-proletarian tongue. It held a similar position to that of Lysenkoism, a now-discredited theory of inherited characteristics in biology. This changed, however, when Stalin turned his hand to linguistics with a *Pravda* article (probably ghost-written) that year, ruling in favour of the Anti-Marrists after the newspaper's surprisingly open debate on the matter. Various theories have been advanced to explain Stalin's linguistic U-turn, but it seems likely to have been motivated less by a desire to rectify a dodgy theory and more by the need to maintain uncertainty across society, on which his rule rested and which was Stalin's *modus operandi*.

[76] Sergei Bobrov (1889–1971), at this time a statistician, but also a painter, poet, novelist and reviewer (including of Mandelstam's second book, *Tristia*); one-time Futurist and early publisher of Pasternak; later exiled to the northern Kazakh town of Kokshetau. The lines may refer to literary work by Bobrov, but the translator was unable to confirm this.

    Fragment from the archive of Alexander Ivich (see note 102), whose daughter Sonia Bogatyryova (born 1932) was stipulated by Nadezhda as her heir and thus Mandelstam's future literary executor. The stipulation was revoked in 1957, however, when this role was transferred to a commission including Akhmatova and Khardzhiev (see note 112), tasked with preparing publication of Mandelstam's work when this became possible following the Khrushchev Thaw.

A bearing and a ball [77]
decided they needed a race.
Away the bearing whizzed,
but the ball kept up with its pace.

End of the 1920s

Pomponych, *civis* of Rome [78]
and one of its finest debauchers,
bored by virtue of numerous causes
(senility coming on fast),
invited his friends to his home.
Deciding he no longer needed them,
he slit the tendons of tedium:
his spirit gave one last moan
and rejoined the steam from the bath.

End of the 1920s

---

[77] A "race" is also the part of a bearing in which a ball rests. From Pavel Luknitsky's archive.

[78] The Nerler edition includes an ironic dedication to Fyodor Panfyorov (1896–1960), novelist and at the time one of the leaders of the RAPP (Russian Association of Proletarian Writers), who were hostile to Mandelstam, styling him and Akhmatova as hangovers from pre-revolutionary Russia. The basis for this dedication is a comment in the typescript referring to Panfyorov's invention of a compound pun translated here as the "tendons of tedium". From Pavel Luknitsky's archive.

In the 1950s, Panfyorov was to lose his position as a literary functionary for having published a book review emphasizing the grassroots nature of the Soviet partisans during the Second World War, rather than the Party's role in the *ad hoc* military units behind Nazi lines.

Visionary raving from Sinai to Tabor [79]
about your covenants, you sign one more.

1920s (?)

Ubi bene, ibi patria, ancients tend [80]
to say. But since the day Ben Livshits became my friend,
it's *ibi patria, ubi bene* I say to them.

Second half of the 1920s

---

[79] *Sinai*: mountain in the south of Egypt's Sinai peninsula, where Moses received the Ten Commandments. *Tabor*: mountain in northern Israel, where Jesus was transfigured.
 Recorded by Nadezhda Mandelstam and preserved in the Princeton archive. According to her, dedicated to David Vygodsky (1893–1943), poet, translator, neighbour of Benedikt Livshits, friends with the Mandelstams. He was the cousin of the influential developmental psychologist Lev Vygotsky (who changed the "d" in his surname to "t" to avoid confusion with his literary cousin). David Vygodsky died in the Gulag, having been arrested at the same time as Livshits in the 1938 "Translators' Case", in which a number of translators were accused of counter-revolutionary activity.
 This translation complements the one that appeared in *Concert at a Railway Station* ("As if some prophet down from talking with the Lord, / gibbering, you lumber towards your next award.").

[80] *Ubi bene, ibi patria*: a rough translation from Cicero's Latin (derived from Aristophanes' Greek) might read "Where life is cool, that's home". *Ben Livshits*: see note 60. Preserved by Livshits's widow, Yekaterina Livshits (1902–1987; in the Gulag from 1940 to 1947), who pointed out that, in contrast to many other writers in the post-revolutionary years, her husband and Mandelstam were against emigrating from the Soviet Union.

Some Jew in the Junior Communists chose [81]
to paint us the past. But words mutate:
his bells still jingling, our historian relates,
one landowner's *deed* was to hurry off straight
to *liquidity* there at the staging post.

1920s (?)

[Two poems on fur] [82]

She's long been huntin' Siberian furs, has Mrs. Karanovich.
What a lodger she's got herself though, and on the Pokrovka! Totally skint!
"Gran, the fur coat's off!" the panting grandson once screamed over,
"That Mandelstam don't give a monkey's about your mink!"

*

---

[81] According to Yekaterina Livshits (see preceding note), an epigram for Iosif Utkin (1903–1944), who was a poet, journalist and member of the *Komsomol* (Young Communist League), later to die in a plane crash holding, apparently, a book of poems by Lermontov. In the original poem, the satirized writer thinks that the word for "mortgage deed" means "coach and horses" and that the word for "a fresh order of post horses" means "country road".

Included in the Mets and Nerler editions following the earlier Struve/Filipoff edition.

[82] For two months the Mandelstams rented a room in Moscow from a Mrs. Karanovich. Leaving behind her mother and son, she had gone to Siberia to work and/or because she'd heard that furs were cheap there (Nadezhda Mandelstam's and Emma Gerstein's accounts differ slightly on this). The Mandelstams failed to pay their rent. Nadezhda Mandelstam recorded the first poem in her memoirs, framing it as a dialogue between the poet and their frequent visitor the actor Vladimir Yakhontov (1899–1945; he committed suicide fearing imminent arrest, according to her). Emma Gerstein recorded the second poem in her memoirs, likewise recalling that the poet and Yakhontov would read both poems dramatically in parts whenever the latter came to visit the Mandelstams.

During the Second World War, Yakhontov solo-funded the manufacture of a Red Army tank on condition it be named the "Vladimir Mayakovsky" (Yakhontov was a keen Mayakovsky reciter). The tank took part in the final attack on Berlin.

I'd love to, Granny K.,
but I'll need to know (please note)
whether to pull on my DJ
or my fanciest fur coat.

1931

Lo! In Khalatov The Caliph's gardens, [83]
we scented the Genesis story,
and who didn't savour that fragrance departing
from *Land and Factory*? The glory
of all these pipsqueaks, all their praise
must still be sung without fail,
and there on the rose of *Artlit* he sways,
doth Comrade Nightingale.

Early 1931 (?)

---

[83] Artemy (Artashes) Khalatov (1894–1938, shot) was an Armenian from Baku, the capital of Azerbaijan. At this time, he ran *Gosizdat*, which oversaw all Soviet publishing politically. The "izdat" part of this portmanteau word may be familiar from *samizdat*, the self-publishing practised by non-conformist writers in the late period of the Soviet Union. Emma Gerstein relates Mandelstam's own account of having been kept waiting at Khalatov's office and seeing other writers be called in before him. When Katayev (see note 57) arrived and was called in straight away, Mandelstam stormed off with the words "I am a Russian poet!", and slammed the door.

Artlit renders here the State Publishers of Artistic Literature (whose Russian abbreviation was *GIKhL*; renamed *Goslitizdat* in 1934). This organization had been formed by spinning off a department of *Gosizdat* and merging it with the publisher Land and Factory (*Zemlya i fabrika*; see the introduction for this publisher's role in the Gornfeld Affair). Vasily Solovyev (1890–1939) was *GIKhL*'s first head manager and a prominent Bolshevik. His surname means the bird referred to in the poem.

Recorded by Sergei Rudakov in a letter to his wife in 1936.

[The Vermel poems] [84]

EPIGRAM IN TERCETS [85]

On Great Nikita Street you'll see
the house in which that Yuli Vermel,
star pupil of Barbey d'Aurevilly,

hides out with his zoological clique.
A total snob, the illustrious Barbey
engendered more than a little critique

by leaving his stamp on his protégé.
What Barbey wore? Well, who can tell.
I doubt that any English kid

has asked their granddad whether to say
"Darby" or "Dareby". As for Vermel,
Barbey's frock coat is no bad fit.

Spring 1931

*

---

[84] Yuli Vermel (1906–1942(?), died in the Gulag), biologist and friend of both Mandelstam and Boris Kuzin (1903–1973), to whom Mandelstam's poem 'To the German Language' is dedicated. With Kuzin, he co-authored *Outlines of Evolutionary Theory* (Moscow: 1924).

The first three poems of this cycle were preserved by the critic Yevgeny Arkhippov (1880/1–1950) having been passed on by the poet Vera Merkureva (1876–1943). The fourth was preserved by Kuzin. The fifth and sixth originate, without further available bibliographical information, from a 1991 publication (in Russian) entitled 'Dante and the Cabby' (see below for the "Fable" of the same name).

[85] Jules Barbey d'Aurevilly (1808–1889), author of *On Dandyism and George Brummell* (the latter an English Regency-era male fashion guru). Barbey's book became the manifesto of Dandyism. Kuzin gave the sartorially *engagé* Vermel a copy (ironically, it seems) in an unsuccessful attempt to get the latter out of his habits, as it were.

Huffing and puffing, to and fro
Vermel goes hunting an embryo:
for a decent booksleeve, what's nice and firm is
a specimen snipped from the human epidermis.
So like a burglar, he looks and looks
for the hide of a cleaner to bind his book.
The skin of women, the skin of kids
are soft as the gloves of militarists…
He almost chokes from all this sex
in his stuffy office of study objects.

October 1932

*

"I despair of Moscow and I have [86]
departed," he wrote, "for Gatchina."
Vermel's a kind of Chaadayev
with a different dream: to snatch in a
second, from out of the womb
of his brother's beloved wife –
well, you'll be thinking, whom?
What theory's he bringing to life?
For a binding, a nephew or niece
has all the dermal wherewithal!
And he pinches that little beast,
like a girl at the coats in a hall.

October 1932

---

[86] Pyotr Chaadayev (1794–1856), Russian philosopher critical of what he saw as his country's inward-looking historical course. The latter has frequently been identified with Moscow, deep inland, in contrast to St. Petersburg, on the Baltic seaboard. Gatchina is a town near St. Petersburg and was one of the imperial residences. In a blend of Westernizer and Slavophile discourse, Mandelstam's 1914 essay on Chaadeyev praises him for finding something in the West that only Russia can fully achieve. See introduction, III, for further comments on the inclusion of this and the preceding poem.

Vermel knew all the cantilevers
supporting all that thought of Kant's.
Frock-coated, black bow-tied, his stance
was that of absolute believers.
More than merely a reasoning pup,
regarding every word of Immanuel's,
Yuli Vermel really knew his spaniels.
But Kant The Spaniel would gobble him up.

1932 (?), ascribed

*

Requiring a hat, Vermel went down
to Dmitrov. That hat he bought was quite a
matter of awe to the whole of the town:
less of a hat, and more of a mitre.
Vermel and hats! How well he picks 'em!
He gave his parents a right parade!
There's a hat shortage though in the Soviet system,
and minus his hat, back home he strayed.

1932 (?), ascribed

*

His sleep is serene.
August. No snow
or ice to be seen.
It's April, though…
At the family funeral,
the guests in the room are all
looking round quickly:
there's a spook in a trilby.

1932 (?), ascribed

A stallion meowed, a tomcat neighed – [87]
this Jew's design is Kazakh-made.

1932 (?)

The Prince of Zvenigorod (fourteenth century) [88]
scoffed seventy pancakes at just one sitting.
Now poor Prince Andrei feels less than fit:
how it batters away, that ancestral memory.

1932

---

[87] Addressed to Pavel Vasilyev (1910–1937), a poet originally from Semipalatinsk in Kazakhstan. At this time, he would often visit Mandelstam at the Herzen House in Moscow, where the Mandelstams were living. According to Emma Gerstein, the corridor gossip was that Vasilyev was under Mandelstam's influence. As with so many of this book's residents, Vasilyev's own fate was to be tragic: arrested in 1934 for drunkenness, hooliganism, breaking the internal passport rules, anti-Semitism, whiteguardism and defending the kulaks, he was rearrested in 1937 on the charge of being part of a terrorist conspiracy to murder Stalin, and shot.

Included in the Mets and Nerler editions following the earlier Struve/Filipoff edition.

[88] Andrei Zvenigorodsky (1878–1961), poet and friend of Mandelstam at this time, had indeed been a prince before the Revolution. In a 1925 diary entry, the poet-critic Nikolai Ashukin (1890–1972) describes him as living off porridge oats and having not even enough money for tea. *Zvenigorod*: small, historical town near Moscow, prominent in the 14th century.

Included in the Mets and Nerler editions following the earlier Struve/Filipoff edition.

The Marguletics [89]

1
Margulis The Old is from Rostov
and a man that Comrade B. recommends,
not just a contemporary of M. Kozakov,
but one of Ostrover and Zhivov's friends. [90]

2
Margulis The Old's increased
our historical sense of the East,
but Madame Shaginyan is better
by far at the *historietta*. [91]

---

[89] Alexander Morgulis (as Mets has it: his surname's spelling may or may not have been confused with a variant spelling in the process of textual transmission) (1898–1938, died in a labour camp in the Soviet north-east). In 1919 he joined the Caucasus department of the Russian Telegraph Service, and later headed its Persian department in the city of Rasht (now in Iran), then part of the short-lived Persian Soviet Socialist Republic established in the area of Gilan from June 1920 to September 1921. From 1927 onwards, he visited and befriended the Mandelstams. In 1931 he was appointed to a position in a newspaper whose name translates as "For Communist Enlightenment" (the organ of the Education Commission), rendered here as *Red Education*. At the end of the 1920s, he started translating.

[90] *Comrade B*: Andrei Bubnov (1884–1938). From 1929 to 1937, head of the Education Commission in the Russian Soviet Federative Socialist Republic (Russia proper incorporating the territories of various minorities, and what is now the Russian Federation). Arrested thirteen times before the Revolution, he took a variety of political positions post-Revolution, and became a member of the Politburo. He was arrested in 1937, sentenced to death in 1938 and shot the same day; his relatives were still searching for him in psychiatric hospitals in the 1970s. Kozakov, Ostrover and Zhivov: Soviet writers.

[91] Marietta Shaginyan (1888–1982), Soviet writer of Armenian descent, born in Moscow, whose published works included the 1913 poetry collection *Orientalia* and some innovative fiction in the 1920s. The latter was criticized as bourgeois decadence, resulting in her reaching out for the party line and writing some books about Lenin. These, however, also ran into trouble when she revealed Lenin's Kalmyk heritage, which a Nazi newspaper picked up on. Mandelstam asked her to intervene on behalf of his friend Boris Kuzin (see note 84) when Kuzin was arrested in 1933.

3
Some demon told me Margulis had made
a splendid jacket for B., our Comrade.
Suddenly the dream switched round midway:
Margulis ran off in our Comrade's DJ.

4
Margulis is down the Education Commission,
but science and tourism aren't his mission.
He's off to Efros for translatees,
that source of the Tigris, whence springeth the Euphrates. [92]

5
Margulis The Old has eyes
that haunt my imagination,
where I read, to this pupil's surprise,
the latest *Red Education*.

6
Margulis The Old – his eyes
don't match his job designation.
One day they're going to organize
his exit from *Red Education*.

7
Margulis The Old, what a traitor!
Oh yes, behind my back
he led my wife down the beaten track
and into a slimy newspaper.

And bar my indignation,
there's little profit, all told,

    In Nadezhda Mandelstam's memoirs, Shaginyan does not come off well, not least because her journalism became implicated in the Purges.

[92] Abram Efros (1888–1954): art historian and translator in charge of the French department at the publishers *GIKhL* (see note 83), and therefore of awarding translation contracts.

from such a snub. Oh may his soul
rest in *Red Education*.

8
His preferences are on and off:
he eats his eggs hard-boiled, then soft.
His cheeky haters all bombard
the world with the lie that Margulis is hard.

9
Margulis The Old. It's only fair
that he lives with Semeyko on Trumpet Square.
And being somebody no one kids,
Margulis lives there, without any kids. [93]

10
Think into the margarite: that molecule is
asleep deep down in the fertile earth.
The summer stars shine on. More worth
lies in that fossil we call Margulis. [94]

1927–1932

---

[93] Nikolai Semeyko: writer, no further information available.
[94] Margarite: $CaAl2(Al2Si2)O10(OH)2$, brought on as substitute here for the original's *marganets* (manganese).

Individual poems recorded variously in the memoirs of Nadezhda Mandelstam and Emma Gerstein as well as in a 1949 edition of the emigré journal *Grani* ("Borderlands", or perhaps "Dividing Lines"), edited by Nikolai Polyakov, or by this time Osipov, a pseudonym adopted by him and his wife Olimpiada Polyakova (Lydia Osipova) (1902–1958). As active Nazi collaborators, they changed their names to avert extradition from Germany, where they had ended up in 1945. Her *Diary of a Collaborator* (1954) begins on 22 June 1941, the day the Nazis invaded the Soviet Union, stating "However bad the Germans are, they won't be worse."

Margulis the Old would sing us [95]
Beethoven down the avenue…

1920s (?)

Young Manuilov, round he goes [96]
among the gigantic buffaloes.

Late 1920s–early 1930s

Not as a wave on some Greek sea, [97]
or like a toad on Witches' Night,
I picture myself (no, I don't feel right)
in a women's jail as a detainee.

---

[95] From a "Marguletic" about Morgulis's habit of singing complex Beethoven melodies while out walking. Nadezhda Mandelstam was unable to fully recall this poem; fragment preserved by Pavel Luknitsky.

[96] Recorded by its subject, Viktor Manuilov (1903–1987), a friend of Alexander Morgulis (see preceding poems). As a young literary scholar, he met Mandelstam in the foyer of a concert hall, Mandelstam delivering this impromptu.

[97] Recollected by Olga Ovchinnikova, who worked as a criminal psychologist at the Novinskaya Women's Prison in Moscow. Mandelstam wrote this after several conversations with her. Nerler's one-stanza version from Nadezhda Mandelstam's notes includes a dedication "To Olga Ovchinnikova, Police Girl".

Though it plays no direct role in the poem, Mandelstam must have been aware of an incident in 1909 connecting the worlds of incarceration and poetry. Two years after the prison had opened, a group of women escaped with the help of a warder, Alexandra Tarasova, who was a member of the Socialist Revolutionary Party (with which the young Mandelstam briefly sympathised). They were wearing escape clothes sewn by Vladimir Mayakovsky's mother and sister, the 16-year-old future Futurist himself ringing a bell from a nearby church as the signal for the escape to begin. Three of the thirteen escapees were immediately recaptured; not exactly inexplicably, Tarasova lost her job, but no further punishment is recorded. Mayakovsky was arrested and released after half a year for lack of evidence.

And this keeps rolling through my brains.
I've long known what will surely ensue:
that one day I'll catch sight of you
as I'm escorted inside in chains.

Late 1920s–early 1930s

I'm a man who's not from here, [98]
oh Lesbos is my home,
yes I'm a Lesbosonian,
but Lesbos is nowhere near.

Early 1930s

How long's it been now since GUM sold [99]
you to me, hat? Ten years, at least.
I'm peering out and looking old
beneath your flaps, a bearded priest.

Around 1932

---

[98] This poem resurfaced in 1994 in an issue of the literary journal *Novy Mir* in which Mikhail Ardov (son of the Ardovs, close friends of Akhmatova) relayed this text, as recalled by the poet and dramatist Mikhail Volpin (1902–1988, sentenced in 1933 to five years in the Gulag for writing satirical verses, of which he served three and a half). A further version preserved by the poet Arseny Tarkovsky (1907–1989, father of *Stalker* director Andrei Tarkovsky) is entitled 'The Song of the Free Cossack'.

[99] *GUM*: famous department store on Moscow's Red Square. The poem was found on the back of a photo showing Mandelstam in the hat in question, together with Nadezhda Mandelstam and the artist Eleonora Gurvich (1890–1989), married to his brother Alexander; some of her work hangs in the Tretyakov Gallery in Moscow, and her teachers included Vladimir Favorsky (1886–1964), the graphic artist and book illustrator referred to in the Voronezh poem "Copper and wood describe Favorsky's flight". The photo in question is readily locatable with internet searches, though Gurvich is usually cropped out.

Where the wilds went over to arable, [100]
the irrigation would gurgle.
And where those ditches gurgle,
you'll now find grazing cattle.
And where there are grazing cattle,
the elderly man will warble.

1934 (?)

---

[100] According to Nadezhda Mandelstam, addressed to Suleyman Stalsky (1869–1937, died of natural causes), farmer and poet-singer of the Lezgins, a people inhabiting parts of the Caucasus. Their language has 18 grammatical cases and 54 consonants. From 1934, he was national poet of the Dagestan Autonomous Soviet Socialist Republic, on whose territory a majority of the Lezgins lived (and continue to do so, in today's Republic of Dagestan, part of the Russian Federation). Gorky called him the "Homer of the twentieth century". Though there's no reason to doubt the authenticity of his early work, arising from decades of manual labour, by the 1930s he had become part of Stalinism's ideological machine – or better, organism, given its dynamism. A photo apparently exists of Stalin listening to Stalsky perform at the All-Union Congress of Cattle Breeders. From Pavel Luknitsky's archive.

The waters of Phlegethon lap, [101]
and the vaults of Tartarus shake.
We've scoffed the entire cake,
Pyast's well-set poison trap.[102]

Early 1934

---

[101] *Phlegethon*: a river of fire in the Greek underworld. *Tartarus*: the dungeon of Hades, used *inter alia* to incarcerate the Titans. These first two lines quote Pushkin's 1824 poem 'Proserpina' (Mets notes that these two lines got distorted in scribal recollection; the translation resorts in part to one of these distortions).
[102] Vladimir Pyast (1886–1940, died of lung cancer, or possibly suicide) was a Symbolist poet but an early admirer and friend of Mandelstam, with whom he was closely associated in many contemporaries' minds. He was internally exiled to Archangelsk and then the Vologda region in Northern Russia for three years, where he composed some long poems (prefiguring Mandelstam's 1934 to 1937 internal exile to Voronezh which was to yield *The Voronezh Workbooks*). Returning to Moscow in 1934, he lived for a while with the Mandelstams. Lev Gumilyov (see note 107) also lived briefly with the Mandelstams at this time, and told Mets in 1975 that they were all hungry during this period. The one thing they did not want to eat was something sweet, as it would only hurt the stomach still further.

The poem was preserved by the writer, journalist and children's author Alexander Ivich (1900–1978, born Ignaty Bernshteyn). His mother was Stefan Zweig's Russian translator and his father a railway engineer in the Far East who died in the 1900 Boxer Rebellion. During World War II, Ivich was the military correspondent of the Black Sea Fleet's aviation arm. In 1949 he was denounced as the "Enemy No. 1 of children's literature". In 1922 he had been entrusted with the poet Vladislav Khodasevich's papers when the latter left Russia, and in 1946 Nadezhda Mandelstam placed in his keeping the most comprehensive collection of Mandelstam's hitherto unpublished work, which became the basis of Mandelstam's posthumous publications.

I hear Pyast's rapid steps on the stairs, [103]
Scrap 75 pokes onto his coat.
My soul in confusion, I scent the Edam,
could relieve him of five full cigarette packs.

Early 1934

Two translators once fell upon us [104]
and summoned us round to follow them
one last time as they marched in a column
with Oedipus at Colonus.

1934

---

[103] *Pyast*: see preceding note. *Scrap 75*: the long poems Pyast had worked on in internal exile had sections he called "*Otryvy*", a word with several viable translations, most literally "tear-offs".

My soul in confusion, I scent quotes and repurposes Pushkin's 1830 poem 'On a Translation of the Iliad', consisting in a pair of hexameters:

I hear the sound of heaven's Hellenic speech that fell quiet;
my soul in confusion, I scent the old man's tremendous shadow.

Pushkin's couplet likely refers to an 1829 translation of the *Iliad* by Nikolai Gnedich (1784–1833), the first full verse translation of Homer's epic into Russian. The translation took Gnedich twenty-two years, including six years of initial work that he ditched on becoming convinced that he really should be doing the job in hexameter rather than alexandrine. Pushkin seems to have been ambivalent about the translation; he was on record as praising it, but also lampooned Gnedich in another poem.

Preserved in Maria Shkapskaya's album.

[104] Nadezhda Mandelstam, who records this poem in her memoirs, related how Sergei Shervensky (1892–1991), poet and translator, had invited Mandelstam and Akhmatova to hear a translation of Sophocles' play *Oedipus at Colonus* by Vladimir Nilender (1883–1965). The two poets, according to Nadezhda, did not treat the reading with the gravity expected of them.

The old apocryphon that I recall [105]
is where a maned Leviathan once chased
Maria round a dust and stone-filled waste,
since Joseph knew no jealousy at all.

That patriarch believed – bit of an oddball –
Maria to be proud, his trust well-placed:
she said he lived off manna, that cub she faced,
and she'd no need of any other soul.

She's got so tender in the interim,
her love, my God, has wandered so wide, and
her desert's now so short of sand

that red and amber hair have simply mingled,
and now those claws that she would once withstand
have left their scratches on her linen skin.

Early 1934

---

[105] Maria Petrovykh (1908–1979), poet and translator from several Eastern European and Soviet languages; close associate of Akhmatova and Mandelstam; her husband died in the Gulag in 1942. At the time this sonnet was written, Lev Gumilyov was staying with the Mandelstams. His first name means "lion", while Osip Mandelstam's first name is the Russianized form of Joseph, a fact he played with more than once, such as in "Poisoned bread, not a drop in the air", or, more surreptitiously, in "My weapon's the vision of thin-bodied wasps" (see *Concert at a Railway Station* and *The Voronezh Workbooks* respectively). Both gentlemen were seeking a relationship with Petrovykh at this time, according to Emma Gerstein.

Apocryphon: Chapter 19 of the *Gospel of Pseudo-Matthew* (also known as *The Infancy Gospel of Matthew*, and in earlier times as *The Book About the Origin of the Blessed Mary and the Childhood of the Saviour*), begins: "Lions and panthers adored Him likewise, and accompanied them in the desert. Wherever Joseph and the blessed Mary went, they went before them showing them the way, and bowing their heads; and showing their submission by wagging their tails, they adored Him with great reverence. Now at first, when Mary saw the lions and the panthers, and various kinds of wild beasts, coming about them, she was very much afraid." (from an 1886 translation by various hands).

Unjealously recorded by Nadezhda Mandelstam and preserved by Alexander Ivich.

She's sitting there with well-parched lips, [106]
all her breath in the groans she repeats.
Maria seems to have strained her hips
to bear these twins – two theatre seats.

Winter 1933–1934

---

[106] *Maria*: see preceding note. From a typescript in the Princeton archive of Mandelstam's work. See introduction, III, for further comments on the inclusion of this and similar poems.

The Bolsheviks love lifts: a fact. [107]
The French adore the lofty style.
Come on, make me dictator! I'll
teach that Lev Gumilyov some tact.

Winter 1933–1934

---

[107] Lev Gumil<u>yo</u>v (1912–1992), a thoroughly tragic and controversial figure, and a vortex for many of the lives touched upon in Mandelstam's occasional verse. Half-orphaned when his father, Mandelstam's co-Acmeist and close friend Nikolai Gumilyov, was shot by the Bolsheviks in 1921 for involvement in an alleged counter- revolutionary conspiracy, Lev Gumilyov spent fourteen years in the Gulag from 1938 through to 1956 (with a break in the middle to take part in the Battle of Berlin). Acting as the authorities' leverage over his mother, Anna Akhmatova, he also seems to have had enough difficulties of his own with them. Reproaching her for having done too little to secure his release (and their relationship had been periodically distant before this anyway), he would eventually break off contact with her, rejecting for example her 'Requiem' cycle, which references his own fate, as self-mythologization on her part. In his own 'Auto-obituary' he later wrote: "Why perform the last rites on someone you could phone?" Biographers are still picking apart the question of who the guilty party in the mother/son estrangement was: in 1955 (while Lev was still in the Gulag) Akhmatova made her third husband's daughter rather than Lev Gumilyov her heir, suggesting – depending on how you look at it – either cold-heartedness or a hard practical necessity. A possible rapprochement (facilitated by Nadezhda Mandelstam) at the end of Akhmatova's life was thwarted when she died in 1966.

As Mandelstam's four-liner suggests, Lev Gumilyov seems indeed to have lacked tact (or more closely, *skromnost'*, "modesty" in the original), badly concealing the elitist attitudes with which he had been brought up and which were at odds with the new ideological environment. He had both literary and ethnographic interests: his memoirs (excerpted on the Russian Wikipedia page, a well-written and duly sourced 25,000 words as of December 2020) record the following, during his second spell in the Gulag:

> It's general knowledge that it was categorically forbidden to make any kind of notes in the camp. I went to the camp boss, and knowing his most dominant character traits – issuing warnings and banning things – immediately went for the maximum. "Would it be possible for me to write?" – "What do you mean by 'write'?" frowned the sleuth. "Translating poems and writing a book about the Huns." – "Why do you want to do that?" he asked back. "So that I won't have to get involved in all the gossip, and to feel calmer, pass the time and not cause any bother, either for myself or for you." Looking at me suspiciously, he spoke: "I'll think about it." Several days later he called me in and said: "Yes to the Huns; no poetry."

Despite his long periods of incarceration, he was later able to pursue an ongoing if precarious scholarly career combining history, geography, philology and archaeology (including scuba diving, when he went to find the base of a Sassanid wall in the Caspian Sea), also collaborating with biologists such as Mandelstam's friend Boris Kuzin. His terminology included *passionarnost'* ("passionarity") to describe the supposed waxing and waning urge of a group (especially its leaders) to geographically and politically expand over the course of the group's "ethnogenesis", the high point of which he described (echoing his parents' literary affiliation) as its "acmatic" phase.

His work has become associated with Eurasianism, which sees Russia's history (and future) as being bound up primarily with the Turkic and Mongol peoples of Asia. This might be viewed as a kind of uber-Slavophilia, or orientophilia, ratcheting up still further the long debate in Russia between Westernizers and Slavophiles. That debate has its first rumblings with Peter the Great's construction of St. Petersburg as "a window through to Europe" (as Pushkin writes in his mid-length poem 'The Bronze Horseman', translated by the present translator in a 2011 edition from Longbarrow Press), becomes fully articulated in the 19th century, and continues to this day. Originally developed by anti-Soviet Russian emigrés in the 1920s and 30s, the Eurasia theory enjoyed a new surge of interest in the 1980s, Lev Gumilyov describing himself as "the last Eurasianist".

The theory has proven appealing to the geopolitical practice of current autocrats east of the Vistula: there's now a Lev Gumilyov University in the city formerly known as Astana (the St. Petersburg – or better Brasilia – of Kazakhstan) and renamed Nur-Sultan after multi-term president Nursultan Nazarbayev moved to an advisory role in 2018. And in a piece of minor historical irony – emblematic of the intertwining of Russia's twin political traditions of autocracy and dissidence – the idea's been picked up and strategically deployed by an ex-employee of the organization that sent Lev Gumilyov's father to the firing squad and Mandelstam to the Gulag: Vladimir Putin. Notwithstanding Lev Gumilyov's close relationship with Mandelstam in his formative years (and his very on-off relationship with Emma Gerstein, who was also Jewish), his work has been criticized not only for Social Darwinism and determinism but also for anti-Semitism: the mobility of Eastern nomads is valorized while that of Jewish merchants is problematized (at the very least, his ideas easily lend themselves to essentialism, and there is clear attestation of hostility to individual Jews in his later years). In this respect, it's hard not to see Mandelstam (more or less a Westernizer, *après le mot*) as a father figure against whom Lev Gumilyov would later rebel.

Academic reception of his work has varied from selective praise of his style and imagination to outright dismissal of his theories, if often from regional specialists reacting to the generalist Gumilyov's encroachment on their territory (in two senses) and/or themselves subject to and negotiating party lines. There have also been accusations of pseudo-science ("a myth-maker in scholar's clothing", wrote the archaeologist Lev Klejn in 1992). If nothing else, he can be seen as a distinctive

That isn't the tail of a foal in a fit [108]
but Jascha The Kid at his violin.
Jascha is back! And no other kid
delivers a foal such a kick in the shin!

1934

---

iteration of the non-Western intellectual reacting to the historical hegemony of the West, as Pankaj Mishra elaborates in *From the Ruins of Empire* and *Age of Anger*.
The poem is preserved in the Russian State Archive of Literature and Art.
[108] Jascha Heifetz (1901–1987), virtuoso violinist, left Russia for the U.S. in 1917. Mandelstam had seen Heifetz play as a child prodigy, and heard him play again when he performed in Russia in 1934. The poem was recorded by Tatyana Grigoryeva (1901–1981), entomologist and second wife of Mandelstam's youngest brother Yevgeny; she accompanied the poet to the concert. Mandelstam was a keen concert-goer, writing two more concert-inspired poems within a year of this piece, "Like a hectic Gypsy throng" and "Once upon a time, Voronezh", and in 1937, "Iota and theta, the flute" (see *The Voronezh Workbooks*), as well as the 1921 poem 'Concert at a Railway Station'.

I'd so like to see you a few decades later, [109]
Maria, a doddery-headed translator
tirelessly shuffling off to a new
minority, who've been expecting you.
Without the requirement to file a request,
you'd call on your publishers, eminent guest,
and emerge, from behind Shengeli's pine door,
with gifts from Ukrainians you couldn't find rhymes for.

Early 1934

---

[109] Addressed (and read) to Maria Petrovykh (see note 105), who was working on translations from Lithuanian and Ukrainian at the time; she later recalled that she found it particularly difficult to translate from the latter precisely because of its linguistic proximity to Russian. *Shengeli*: see note 74. At the time, he was chief editor for the poetry of the peoples of the USSR at the publishers *Goslitizdat* (the renamed *GIKhL*). Preserved, in slightly varying forms, in the archives of Alexander Ivich and Pavel Luknitsky.

The keeper comes, they buzz their wings. [110]
It's that kind of species, the bee.
Who's counted Anna Akhmatova's stings
for twenty-three years? Just me.

February 1934

---

[110] Preserved by Pavel Luknitsky. The poem echoes the third stanza of a 1912 poem by Akhmatova, who first met Mandelstam in 1911:

FRAGMENT

...Then something rustled, a fallen leaf
where the forest felt no sun:
"That man you love, confess what he's
been doing," it said, "what he's done!

It seems some dark mascara has
increased your eyelids' weight.
He's given you up to love, that assassin:
you're choking, your muscles ache...

You've long since given up counting stings,
your breast quite dead from those needles.
Forget about joy! Just settle right in
to your grave while you still breathe."

"You're dark and devious," I said, "enough!
You bully! Learn some shame!
He's quiet and tender, obedient, his love
won't ever desert me again."

Along the shores of seas [111]
where once there sailed the Argives,
the Archivians live, a nation
truly among the most ancient.
Their barbarous trade is in archives,
flogging them off to Authorities.
The page is what they feed on,
as it quivers away, all sacred;
they devour foul-rustling leaves.
Held in contempt, and naked –
how sad! But what is their game?

1934

---

[111] In 1934, Mandelstam and other writers were contacted by the State Museum of Literature in Moscow, which was asking to purchase their archives. The Mandelstams were, as ever, strapped for cash, but Mandelstam rejected the Museum's offer of 500 roubles, considering it a calculated insult: Mikhail Kuzmin, for example, had sold his archive for 25,000 roubles, according to Ralph Dutli. The poem is dated by an angry letter from Mandelstam to Vladimir Bonch-Bruyevich (1873–1955), founder and head of the Museum and one-time close associate and *de facto* secretary of Lenin.

At the turn of the century, Bonch-Bruyevich had been involved in the resettlement of the persecuted Doukhobor (literally "spirit-wrestler") sect from the Caucasus to Canada (a project organized from London). Slightly later, the sect was to gain notoriety with their naked protests against the Canadian military draft. Bonch-Bruyevich then studied sects more generally, and edited a newspaper targeted at them called *Rassvet* ("Daybreak"), published by the Russian Social Democratic Labour Party (the party already with Bolshevik and Menshevik factions and somewhat later to split entirely).

From an archive of course, in this case Pavel Luknitsky's; also preserved in part by Akhmatova. The first line in Russian (*Na beregu egeyskikh vod*) parodies the start of Pushkin's 'The Bronze Horseman' (*Na beregu pustynnykh voln*).

Enamel, diamonds, plus some gold [112]
Might have met the Egyptians' needs:
My maiden's adorned in twills and tweeds,
All her shape a joy to behold.

1934

---

[112] Recalled by Emma Gerstein (1903–2002), who explained that Lev Gumilyov had given her a photo of himself. While he was writing an acrostic on the back of it, Mandelstam snatched the photo out of his hand, changed one word in what its principal author had written, and supplied the poem's last line (Mandelstam's contribution corresponds more or less to the third line in the translation).

Gerstein had met the Mandelstams in 1928 during a stay at a sanatorium near Moscow, became close friends with them, and was one of those to whom what became known as the Stalin Epigram ("We live, but feel no land at our feet") was read. Nadezhda Mandelstam specifically instructed her to learn it, an act typical of how the Mandelstams tended to treat her, in Gerstein's account. She lived in Moscow her entire life, including during the Nazi bombing and military approach on the city. In the post-war period, she grew closer to Akhmatova and maintained her friendship with Nadezhda Mandelstam, but broke with her in the late 1960s following the latter's dispute with Nikolai Khardzhiev (see note 129) over his editing of the long-awaited first post-Stalin edition of Mandelstam in the Soviet Union (Khardzhiev and Gerstein were also close friends). In addition to the relationship with Lev Gumilyov hinted at in the four-liner, she also had a relationship with Nadezhda Mandelstam's (married) brother and attempted one with Trotsky's son. In the Stalin period, the mark of her association with Mandelstam and Akhmatova precluded permanent positions of employment or advancement. Her research into Lermontov could only be published from the mid-1960s onwards, when she then became a member of the Union of Soviet Writers.

In addition to fascination and admiration, Gerstein's memoirs (perceptively introduced and translated into English as *Moscow Memoirs* by John Crowfoot (London: Harvill Press, 2004)) have attracted doubts and hostility. The curt entry on her in the usually exhaustive Mandelstam Encyclopedia (see Translator's note) seems to be making a point, its brevity only partially down to the fact that autobiography is intermittent and brief in her memoirs (850 pages in the latest Russian edition of 2019). They chiefly document and comment on segments of the lives of others: the Mandelstams, Akhmatova, Lev Gumilyov, Sergei Rudakov, Boris Pasternak, as well as Gerstein's father, who was a physician also consulted by Kremlin leaders. This circumspection also conditions the length of this footnote compared with that on Lev Gumilyov (note 107) and perhaps the two hundred words of the Russian Wikipedia entry as of April 2021 (compared with Lev Gumilyov's 25,000). Describing Gerstein, Yakov Gordin notes: "In cultural history, there are figures whose fate is a paradox. They are long looked upon as witnesses, and they think of themselves as witnesses, but only later does it become clear that they are serious actors in the cultural process in their own right." This applies all the more to those writing from within or about closed societies, as Gerstein was, where official narratives may run very counter to anything like the truth.

I don't need any church in Rome [113]
or gorgeous landscape far from home.
Instead, I'll savour the view of Comrade
Luppol, stood in Jean-Richard's shade.

1934 (?)

---

[113] As with so many of these pieces, the humour of the verse is coloured by the subsequent lives and deaths of those referred to. The poem, recalled by Nadezhda Mandelstam in her memoirs, derives from a newspaper photo of two men.

The first was the philosopher and co-founder of Russian dialectical materialism Ivan Luppol (1896–1943), the then head of the publishers *Goslitizdat*. In 1937, according to Nadezhda Mandelstam, he would tell her husband that the latter would not be getting a line of translation or any other work from the publishers for as long as Luppol was at the editor's desk. He was arrested on fabricated charges in Tbilisi in 1940. His death sentence was commuted to 20 years in the Gulag; he died at a camp in the Urals.

As the poem indicates, Luppol was a great deal shorter than the second man, French writer and communist Jean-Richard Bloch (1884–1947), then visiting the Soviet Union. Some years later, Bloch's 86-year-old mother was murdered upon arrival at Auschwitz (the family was Jewish), and his daughter and son-in-law were executed by the Nazis as active resistance members. "Bloch died suddenly on 15 May 1947, crushed, according to family and friends, by the ordeals, the bereavements and the dramas of the war", says one French source (with thanks to Nick Grindell for locating and translating this).

The errors of ears in keeping abreast [114]
of ideas are as dire as a shortness of breath
for those on the stout side. Let's cite the case
of the linguist who settled down face to face
with one of our less intellectual citizens.
The linguist mentioned the concept of idiom.
In seconds, they were yanking each other's hair.
Whose fault it was here, I think is clear:
the one who felt he'd been physically hit
when he heard the other one call him an idiot.

12 June 1935

That young runt's a right mimosa: [115]
the dainty-eyebrowed git
lives off his boss, Sergei Elozo,
plus eggshell, bit by bit.

3 April 1936

---

[114] Written together with Sergei Rudakov, who enclosed this poem in a letter to his wife (together with "A tailor with a decent head") dated 15 June 1935, writing "Mandelstam and I have collaborated on a fable." Preserved by Emma Gerstein, who suggests it was written after one of Mandelstam and Rudakov's forthright discussions.

[115] Like the previous poem, written together with Sergei Rudakov (though with minimal input from the latter) and preserved by Emma Gerstein. Mandelstam's then flatmate (unnamed) worked for the local Voronezh newspaper *Commune* (still in existence), whose chief editor was Sergei Elozo (1899–1938), active in early attempts to establish television in Voronezh, shot as a member of an alleged "rightist-Trotskyist conspiracy".

The fount of tears has frozen, three stone those shackles weigh – [116]
the ballads mulled in the mind of Rudakov, Sergei.

Late 1936 or early 1937

---

[116] Sergei Rudakov (1909–1944) was a young poet and scholar who befriended and collaborated with Mandelstam in his Voronezh exile in the mid-1930s, himself likewise exiled there. Mandelstam viewed him as his likely later editor. Emma Gerstein's memoir contains a lengthy refutation of Nadezhda Mandelstam's largely negative characterization of Rudakov, though the latter's letters to his wife (excerpted at length in Gerstein's memoir) also reveal a sense of himself going well beyond healthy self-confidence.

Besides Rudakov's enthusiasm for Mandelstam's poetry and their both being Leningraders, their relationship may have been bolstered by the shared experience of people close to them having been shot by the Bolsheviks. In Mandelstam's case, this was Nikolai Gumilyov, and in Rudakov's case, his father and one of his brothers. In one of her many corrective challenges to Nadezhda Mandelstam's narratives, Emma Gerstein writes that Rudakov's father (a general) and his brother initially fought on the White side in the Russian Civil War but went over to the Reds. When required by an investigative commission to publicly distance himself from his Tsarist past, Rudakov's father refused. Rudakov's brother followed their father's lead, and both father and brother were shot. The family tradition of tragic deaths was to continue with Sergei Rudakov himself. Having already served on the Leningrad front early in the Nazi attack on the Soviet Union, he was later sentenced to a punishment battalion for attempting to obtain a draft deferral for an acquaintance. He died on the front near Mogilev, in eastern Belarus.

This poem was recalled by Natasha Shtempel (see next note). In a minor way prefiguring how the Mandelstams would entrust her with part of Osip's later work, Rudakov also deposited some poems with her, which Mandelstam rather nosily found on a visit to Shtempel and her mother's flat, guessing that one of them was dedicated to her. According to Shtempel, it was entitled 'Ballad of Motion', referred to a rafting trip she and Rudakov had taken, and included the phrase "the fount of tears". Rudakov's poem does not appear to have survived in the exact version recalled by Shtempel, but may have been revised and retitled 'Ballad': begun in Voronezh in April/May 1936 and finished in Leningrad in 1938, it includes a raft reference and ends:

The water heard by chance / the jackdaws' midnight trill-sounds. /
The slipshod ballad's founts: / raindrops upon a birch branch.

The phrase "the fount of tears" also appears in the next poem, addressed directly to Shtempel.

Natasha's asleep. A zephyr flies [117]
about her finely coiffured hair.
For girls, as everybody knows

one source of tears is the morning doze,
entailing a decent yell in the ears.
But some great vacuum cleaner dries

her wave with its giant blast of air,
permanently, one might suppose.
Once more it bubbles, that fount of tears.

24 February 1937

---

[117] Surely one of very few poems ever written with the objective of getting someone to change their hairstyle. Natasha Shtempel (1908–1988) notes Mandelstam's unheeded advice to her to drop her marcel wave (a kind of undulating perm) in favour of straight hair. Preserved in the Princeton archive and referred to by its addressee in her memoir 'Mandelstam in Voronezh', originally published in the journal *Novy Mir* in 1987 (as yet untranslated into English).

Shtempel had met and befriended the Mandelstams in Voronezh through Sergei Rudakov, providing important support to them at this time. Shortly before the Mandelstams left Voronezh, she was entrusted with copies of Mandelstam's almost entirely unpublished work from 1930 through to 1937, covering the Moscow period and most of his Voronezh poems. The manuscript was referred to as *Natasha's Book*, which she would preserve through the war years (in which she had to leave Voronezh, which was on the front line; 92% of its buildings were destroyed). She then returned it to Nadezhda Mandelstam, by then Osip Mandelstam's widow.

Unable to pursue doctoral studies because of her aristocratic family background (there had once been a "von" before the "Shtempel"), she spent the late 1920s and early 1930s in a variety of pedagogically related university positions, heading the Vocational Psychology Laboratory of the Institute for Labour Organization and Safety, before becoming a teacher of Russian literature and language at the Aviation College in Voronezh until 1971.

Rural family size is big: [118]
just one can do a full-blown jig.
Vadim won't have us labouring less:
Stoichev – that's his hands-on leader –
spends his days just raising chicks,
but year by year our rabbit breeder
out-Stoichev's him in breeding success.

24 February 1937

---

[118] Vadim Pokrovsky (1909–1987) was a colleague of Natasha Shtempel's at the Institute of Hygiene and Sanitation in Voronezh, where she was working at the time, and later a well-known expert on hygiene. According to Shtempel, he also wrote poems, which were published in Voronezh's literary almanac and a 1933 collection called *The Glorious Life*. She suggested to Mandelstam that she introduce them to each other, to which Mandelstam responded with this poem.

Stepan Stoichev (1881–1938) was the head of Voronezh's teaching college and rumoured to breed poultry, according to Shtempel. He was also head of the Voronezh section of the Union of Soviet Writers, in which capacity he responded to Mandelstam's attempts to obtain financial support by stating: "Let Mandelstam exercise his right to work where and how he wishes to, but not with the Writers' Union". He was arrested in 1937 and executed the following year, having been accused of "rightist-Trotskyist tendencies", of which there seem to have been a lot in Voronezh (see "That young runt's a right mimosa").

Preserved in the Princeton archive.

Lena and Nora erupt like Etna [119]
out of the House of Engineers.
With sour-sweet breath, like Eleanor, Esther,
this pair of ethereal furies appears.

24 February 1937

---

[119] Nora Epstein and her sister Lena were colleagues of Natasha Shtempel at the Institute of Hygiene and Sanitation in Voronezh at this time. Nora's husband was head physician at a hospital and thus a member of the "engineering and technical workers", a stratum of Soviet society with access to better housing. The four-liner may not be quite as caustic in intent as it first appears: Mandelstam knew Lena's husband, an agricultural scientist, from Kiev, visiting him and Lena occasionally. It was on a visit by the Mandelstams to Nora that the poem "Your eyelashes dart, alert and light" (addressed to Nadezhda Mandelstam) in the Second Voronezh Workbook arose.

The Eleanor in question is likely Eleanor of Aquitaine (1122–1204), queen consort initially of France and later England (mother of Richard the Lionheart and John), and a powerful political figure, leading the Second Crusade. In the biblical Book of Esther, Esther is another powerful – if at-risk – figure, being the Jewish queen of the Persian king Ahasuerus. In Greek mythology, the ether is the pure air at the altitudes where the gods dwell.

Recorded by Nadezhda Mandelstam, and discussed in Natasha Shtempel's memoir.

[Four-liners to Natasha Shtempel] [120]

Natasha's back, but where's she been? [121]
She really must eat. She really must drink.
Dark as the night, her mother sniffs.
Her daughter reeks of onions and wine.

*

If God dropped by and thus he spake,
"Natasha, what art thou, my creature?" –
"Lord, I confess, I am a teacher…" –
"Get thee gone", he'd say, "for God's sake!"

*

"Natasha, how would you spell *nitwit*?" [122]
"If I was knitting, I guess with a K."
"*Today*. One word or two." "I've got it!
It's two. Or one? Hmm. I can't say."

*

Oh Natasha, how clumsy of me
to not be Heinrich Heine.
Translating "knob", "sex yob" would be
my choice as rhyme designer.

---

[120] Variously recalled by Nadezhda Mandelstam or Natasha Shtempel, or drawn from authorial manuscripts in the Princeton archive.

[121] *Onions and wine*: According to her memoir, Shtempel in fact hated onions and didn't drink wine.

[122] In her first year of teaching, Shtempel told Mandelstam that during a dictation she was asked whether *v polden'* ("at midday") was written as one word or two. Thinking of the word *polden'* itself ("midday"), which a Russian student might instinctively write as two words, she replied that *v polden'* was written as one word. The resulting error by the entire class was an embarrassment to her, which Mandelstam made fun of (and perhaps tried to alleviate) through this and the preceding poem.

*

Natasha's ordered the next epigram. [123]
I can't keep up! Help! Drag her off me!
One for her mum, for the Sacred Lamb,
and one for Professor P.L. Zagarovsky.

Early 1937, the final four-liner 24 February of that year

A savings-book Trosha has swiped from a library, [124]
that Vadik's eraser took years off, inscribed
for Natasha one day she looked in on her tribe.

1 March 1937

---

[123] Pavel Zagorovsky (1892–1952), psychologist and professor at the Voronezh Institute of Teaching. Shtempel had worked for him while a student there in a group working on paedology, an integrative approach to child development studies championed by Lev Vygotsky (see note 79). The group was shut down in 1935 when paedology and vocational psychology were deemed "pseudoscientific". Zagorovsky and Shtempel became close friends, in part due to a shared interest in literature. He got on well with Mandelstam, who called him "the Velvet Professor".
[124] Mandelstam gave Shtempel a copy of his 1928 edition *Poems* (effectively a New and Collected Poems at the time it was published), inscribing it: "Dear Natasha, I don't know what to write. But I'm glad we've found a book to give you, even if it's a poor one. I promise never again to write such books and to be cooperative in everything – on condition that they'll be cooperative with me too."

The book had indeed been liberated from a library by one Trosha, Sergei Rudakov's flatmate, who worked for the local Institute of Agriculture. The library was at a recuperative facility (a "house of leisure") he had been given leave for, and he had taken the book in order to get it signed by Mandelstam. But Trosha was called off to work in the Voronezh region, and the book was forgotten about. Upon its rediscovery, Mandelstam borrowed an eraser from Vadik, the son of the Mandelstams' landlady at the time, and used it to remove annotations and dirt in the edition, deleting by hand one poem, adding two, changing one or two things, and then gifting the book to Shtempel.

In addition to the poem and accompanying information above, Shtempel noted in her memoir that she would often drop in on her sick uncle after visiting the Mandelstams.

Out of respect for the girl in the maid, the lad took his time [125]
and waited for seventy years to tell the old lady: "I love you!"

Out of respect for the lad in the husband, the maid kept calm
and waited for seventy years to gob in the old git's face.

Between February and May 1937

Decision [126]

If an Egyptian and me got hitched
under the pyramids' legal rules,
I'd buy my wife, my foreign match,
my lady friend, Pyramidon pills.

We'd swim in the Nile and walk the temples,
in summer we'd take our picnic lunch
in the pyramids' shade, and I would fetch
my Lady of the Pyramids her pills.

March (?) 1937

---

[125] A manuscript in the Princeton archive includes a mock title and note: "Translated from the Modern Greek by Osip Mandelstam" and "Found in the archive of an old Greek woman". Other sources lack one or either. Natasha Shtempel wrote that the poem referred to her and Pavel Zagorovsky (see note 123).

[126] *Pyramidon*®: trade-name of the drug Aminophenazon; due to carcinogenic effects, now no longer prescribed. The poem was written on the back of a fragment of the Voronezh poem '[Reims–Laon]' from March 1937 (preserved in the Russian State Archive of Literature and Art), which gives us the dating. Pyramids seem to have been on Mandelstam's mind at the time: see "So that the sandstone, mate of the wind", also from March 1937 (in *Concert at a Railway Station* and *The Voronezh Workbooks*).

Relieved of all tasks when the truth was revealed, [127]
that there wasn't one tool he knew how to wield,
on every question, Hermes was wrong.
Which the Thunder God had known all along.

1930s

As in the primates, there's something which you [128]
may notice in women: an abdominal issue.

Early 1930s, ascribed

---

[127] According to Nadezhda Mandelstam, the poem reflects the removal of Andrei Bubnov (see note 90) from his position as Commissar for Education in 1937.

The text of this poem, drawing on Greek mythology, has been debated to a degree more to be expected of an ancient Greek poem than a modern Russian one. Instead of Hermes, the Messenger, some sources have Hephaestus, the Greek god of metallurgy and crafts, which at first sight makes more sense, given the second line's reference to tools. Mets follows a version in Pavel Luknitsky's archive which has Hermes, however, and mentions communication with Georgy Levinton in 2007. With some vehemence, Levinton views the Hephaestus version as a scribal "improvement" by someone who had not realized the background to the poem: Hermes was the wrong god for the job.

[128] The reader is referred to the introduction, III, for comments on the inclusion of this and similar poems. Included by Mets from a 1992 Moscow edition of Mandelstam, without further sourcing or information.

Gabriel Bloggs adored cigarettes, [129]
but worshipped the Sappho brand.
Efros picked up and heard his request:
"Bring me a smoke, Abraham."

1930s, ascribed

"Is it all quiet down there in the Balkans?" [130]
people would ask the soldier. "Yup,"
he replied, "a cannonball can
blow you to bits, but we all own up."

1930s (?), ascribed

---

[129] Abram Efros: see note 92. The poem is likely an echo of Chapter 29 of Ilf and Petrov's *The Twelve Chairs*, in which a poet attempts to flog a poem to various specialist publications, changing the poem each time to suit its prospective audience, but retaining its central character, Gabriel, a prototypical worker. The chapter's poems spawned their own imitative genre in the 1920s and 30s. There's also an echo in the name, though not in the substance, of Pushkin's famously blasphemous poem 'The Gabriliad'.

Recorded by Nadezhda Mandelstam without her husband's involvement, according to Nikolai Khardzhiev (1903–1996), who edited the first post-Thaw edition of Mandelstam's work.

Some gossip on Khardzhiev and his milieu. Close friends with Emma Gerstein, he was married at one point to Serafima Suok (1902–1983), who was the ex-wife of Mandelstam's co-Acmeist Vladimir Narbut and future wife of the literary theorist Viktor Shklovsky (1893–1984). Khardzhiev's archive included not only manuscripts by Mandelstam, Akhmatova and Khlebnikov but also visual art by the Suprematist Kazimir Malevich, the worth of which ran into millions. The artworks have been the subject of a number of scandals and shady dealings over several decades (in which Khardzhiev was not the guilty party), both before and after Khardzhiev's death. Some has been recovered for the public and for scholarship, some not.

[130] The original refers to and puns on the Battle of Shipka Pass (actually four separate engagements) in the Russo-Turkish War of 1877–1878, in which the Russian Army and Bulgarian volunteers defeated Ottoman forces in central Bulgaria.

Source and date uncertain, included in the Mets edition following an article on Mandelstam published in the U.S. in 1992 by the scholar Sofia Polyakova (1914–1994).

Fables [131]

Once a sub-colonel, ex-White Guards, [132]
who ladies considered a gent,
decided the moment had come
to order himself to go on a personal Lent.
Three or four days then passed
before he munched so much as a crumb.
He fasted so hard
that even his tapeworm came out at last.

---

[131] Some of the earlier fables ('The Fibber and the Fathers', 'Auntie and Mirabeau', 'Dante and the Cabby') were published in journals. Others were variously preserved by Nadezhda Mandelstam or Pavel Luknitsky, and/or appeared in a 1991 publication (in Russian) entitled 'Dante and the Cabby', or the Struve/Filipoff edition. The very last ('A tailor with a decent head') was part of a letter from Sergei Rudakov to his wife in 1935, where Rudakov referred to these poems as 'Foolish Fables', or perhaps 'Fables for Fools'; it's unclear whether this was his or Mandelstam's way of referring to them.

[132] *White Guards*: During the Russian Civil War of (more or less) 1918 to 1921, the White Army opposed the Bolsheviks. Initially, it actually consisted in a number of separate forces, which were then integrated under one command, only to splinter again as defeat approached.

A digression indicative of the times that were to follow this poem's writing: the final White Army outfit was defeated in Siberia in 1923 by a Red Army force led by an officer known as Ivan Strod, which was the Russianized form of his Latvian name, Jānis Strods. The captured White commander, Anatoly Pepelyayev, received a death sentence. Initially, this was commuted to ten years' imprisonment (thereafter extended for three years), after which Pepelyayev worked as a carpenter in Voronezh, the city to which Mandelstam had by then been internally exiled. Re-arrested in 1937 as part of a round-up of former White Guards, however, Pepelyayev was executed in 1938 in Novosibirsk. By then, a certain Red Army officer had also been arrested and executed in Moscow as part of the NKVD's "Latvian Operation" (directed at ethnic Latvians within the Soviet Union's then borders, deemed unreliable because in this period Latvia was an independent country before its re-incorporation into Russian hegemony in 1940). The executed Red Army officer was Ivan Strod / Jānis Strods.

But if fasting were deemed an Olympic event,
the victor would be whoever reads *Our Stronghold Fast* [133]
on an empty tum.

Around 1923

*

The Fibber and the Fathers [134]

It's well known Catholics think
divorce a sin.
An Italian barber made a trip
to the episcopal court to discuss
an important matter regarding
its hairstyle needs.
But from his eyes the dean could suss
that this was a fib:
"My son, leave now in peace.
We will not accept your parting."

1924

*

It seems that they've become so rare, oh [135]
those who respect the departed, today.
Where ancestors quietly fester away,

---

[133] *Our Stronghold Fast* renders the original's *Na Postu*, the name of the organ of the RAPP (see note 78) from 1923 to 1925. The journal's full name was *Na Literaturnom Postu* ('At Our Literary Posts'), its shortened form unintentionally punning, give or take a preposition, on the Russian for "on a fast".

[134] In the original, the potential divorcee offers to build the priests an aquarium, and the text puns the Russian for "to breed" and "to divorce".

[135] For further poems on hats and hat theft, see "How long's it been now since GUM sold" and "Requiring a hat, Vermel went down".

one entered a vault and doffed his sombrero.
Within those ancient walls he gave
the sign of the holy cross, just like on
Sundays, right in front of the icon.
He paid his debt to past generations,
then swilled his nibbles with due moderation
on the train back home. Post-expiration,
he was found on the floor, having gone to the grave.
The thief had robbed him down to his hat.

Readers! Don't drink with men you meet like that!

1924

*

AUNTIE AND MIRABEAU [136]

Gawd, she was loaded that auntie of mine!
Her home was a vault full of silver and china,
various knick-knacks, chests made of oak, oh
Louis-Seize tables, chairs in rococo.
Among all that stuff that was painted and woven,
on a varnished piano presided Beethoven,
held by my aunt in especial esteem.
One time I dropped by – there was the figurine.
Stubborn and proud, she peered at the master
and whispered her words at his bust of plaster.
"Sweetie, look, it's Marat by Mirabeau!"
"Auntie, I'm sorry, I really don't think so!"

---

[136] According to Yekaterina Livshits, Nerler reports, this was co-written with her husband Benedikt Livshits, the latter's aunt having given him a bust of Luther. Jean-Paul Marat (1743–1793) and Honoré Gabriel Riqueti, Count of Mirabeau (1749–1791): French revolutionaries.

If you think that the old will budge, *au revoir*!
"Look at this portrait," she said, "of Marat:
if I recall rightly, it's late Mirabeau."

Reader, I think you'll agree that's not so!

1925

*

DANTE AND THE CABBY [137]

With the pep of the working classes,
a cabby ranted away to Dante,
comparing their circumstances,
both of them freelance of course.
"…Me too, that organ's a fave of mine.
The *Rome*'s my top *ristorante*,
though I'm like you, pure Florentine.
Governor, I'm neither a thug nor a thief!
But it don't matter how much I feed my horses,
eight to ten years, they all come to grief,
and then, chop chop, I restock my resources.
About as long as your Beatrice issue…
Not that I'm trying to diss you
or anything. You're like my old man!
Right now I can take you anywhere, I can.
But do me a favour, when the days get shorter
and stop them raising them bridges this Autumn!"

1925

*

---

[137] In St. Petersburg, some of the major bridges are raised at night, allowing shipping through but depriving hard-working cabbies of potential earnings.

There once was a son of a priest
who loved each loaf of rye
the factory squeezed from its yeast
and popped in his gob. He'd cry
"Thank you, oh Commissar for Grain!"
And came out of the oven the same.

End of the 1920s (?)

*

A farmer from a mudbrick farm
somewhere in deepest Uzbekistan
was buying condoms down the co-op
when, like a hound, out of thin air,
a mullah barged past and then and there
snapped the goods up. God, I could throw up!

1930s (?)

*

Some citizen neither totally plastered [138]
nor wholly sober
installed an organ in his flat.
The instrument thundered, sparking
an immediate meeting of neighbours not down with that.
They called the head of the building, who called over
Sebastian the porter and started barking
at Seb to demolish the organ. Which Seb did,
as well as the teeth of the organ's owner,
that antisocial git.

The problem's not that Seb's a bastard.
The problem, of course, was all that barking.

1934 (?)

*

A tailor with a decent head [139]
was sentenced to be got quite dead.
What could he do?
Ever the pro,
he took out his tape and drew
a line from head to toe.

It turns out he's still with us though.

1 June 1934

---

[138] According to Nadezhda Mandelstam, this poem aroused the interest of OGPU operatives during their search of the Mandelstams' flat in May 1934 when arresting the poet.

[139] Written at Sverdlovsk railway station *en route* to Mandelstam's first point of internal exile, Cherdyn, a small town in the Urals, immediately after his interrogation and torture in the Lubyanka.

www.ingramcontent.com/pod-product-compliance
Lightning Source LLC
Chambersburg PA
CBHW031636160426
43196CB00006B/443